Danilo Mango

MATH Dictionary

DK

DK

LONDON, NEW YORK,
MELBOURNE, MUNICH, and DELHI

Author Judith de Klerk
Designed and edited by Tall Tree Ltd.
Additional editing by Lee Wilson,
Penny Smith, Fleur Star,
Carrie Love, Caroline Stamps
Additional design by Hedi Hunter,
Lauren Rosier
Art director Rachael Foster
Publishing manager Bridget Giles
Production editor Siu Yin Chan
Production controller Claire Pearson
Jacket designer Natalie Godwin
Jacket editor Mariza O'Keeffe
US editor Margaret Parrish

Math consultant Alison Tribley

First published in the United States in 2009 by
DK Publishing
375 Hudson Street, New York, New York 10014

ISBN 978-0-7566-5194-7

Color reproduction by Media Development Printing Ltd., UK
Printed and bound by WKT, China

Discover more at
www.dk.com

Contents

Introduction

Carol Vorderman's Math Dictionary contains everything you need to know to get ahead in elementary school math. Whether you're stuck on symbols or need a hand with homework, the dictionary is here to help.

Inside this dictionary you'll find:
A–Z pages Simple, clear definitions of hundreds of mathematical terms. Photographs, illustrations, and diagrams help explain each term, while working examples show how the term is used in practice. Cross-references to entries on related subjects give extra information.

Fast search index It's quick and easy to find your way around the dictionary using the highlighted words and colored index bars.

Quick reference section Turn to these handy tables to look up symbols, useful number words, prefixes, units of measurement, and how to convert metric and Imperial measures.

How to use the A–Z pages

Main entries are in large, bold type.

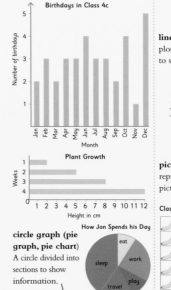

graph

graph
A drawing or diagram that combines information about several things. There are different types of graph.

bar graph Horizontal or vertical bars used to show information. A bar graph with vertical bars or columns is also called a column graph.

Birthdays in Class 4c

Number of birthdays

Jan Feb Mar Apr May Jun Jul Aug Sep Oct Nov Dec
Month

Plant Growth

Weeks

1 2 3 4 5 6 7 8 9 10 11 12
Height in cm

circle graph (pie graph, pie chart)
A circle divided into sections to show information.

How Jon Spends his Day

eat
work
sleep
play
travel

46

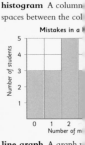

histogram A column spaces between the col

Mistakes in a

Number of students

0 1 2
Number of m

line graph A graph v plot points then join th to show information.

Rainfall

Inches

Jan Feb Mar A
Month

pictograph A graph represent real objects. picture graph or pictog

Class 7b—Favorite Fruit

Subentries of related words are in smaller bold type.

hundreds of entries from abacus to zero

easy-to-read layout

colored panels of expanded entries link related words together

Find out symbols and similar terms at a glance.

Working examples help you to understand how the term is used.

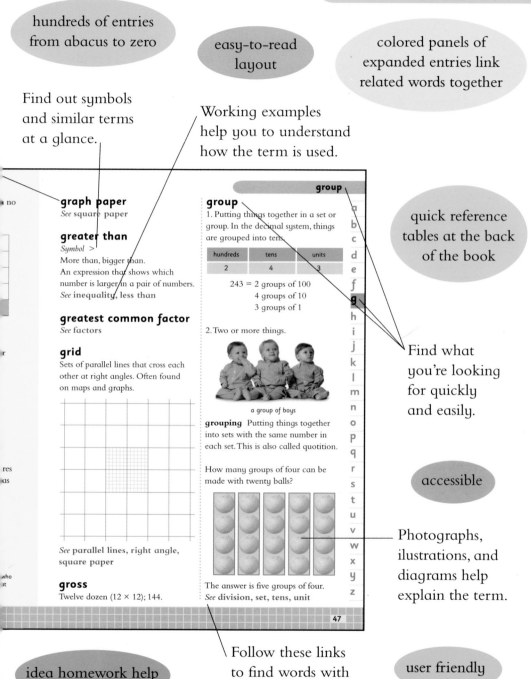

quick reference tables at the back of the book

graph paper
See square paper

greater than
Symbol >
More than, bigger than.
An expression that shows which number is larger in a pair of numbers.
See inequality, less than

greatest common factor
See factors

grid
Sets of parallel lines that cross each other at right angles. Often found on maps and graphs.

See parallel lines, right angle, square paper

gross
Twelve dozen (12 × 12); 144.

group
1. Putting things together in a set or group. In the decimal system, things are grouped into tens.

hundreds	tens	units
2	4	3

243 = 2 groups of 100
4 groups of 10
3 groups of 1

2. Two or more things.

a group of boys

grouping Putting things together into sets with the same number in each set. This is also called quotition.

How many groups of four can be made with twenty balls?

The answer is five groups of four.
See division, set, tens, unit

a
b
c
d
e
f
g
h
i
j
k
l
m
n
o
p
q
r
s
t
u
v
w
x
y
z

Find what you're looking for quickly and easily.

accessible

Photographs, ilustrations, and diagrams help explain the term.

47

Follow these links to find words with related meanings.

idea homework help

user friendly

5

abacus

A counting frame with beads that slide up and down rods. An abacus is used for counting and calculating.

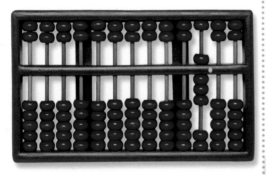

absolute value

Symbol | |

How far a number is from 0 on a number line, on either side of 0. The absolute value of a number is never negative.

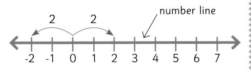

The absolute value of –2 and 2 is 2.

accurate

Exact, correct, without a mistake.
See **approximation**

acute

Sharp. Sharply pointed.

acute angle A sharply pointed angle that is less than a right angle.

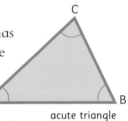

right angle   acute angle

acute triangle

A triangle that has three acute inside angles.

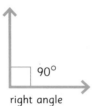

acute triangle

See **angle, triangle**

addition

add, adding

Symbol +

Joining two or more numbers together to make a larger number.

$2 + 3 = 5$

$20 + 30 = 50$

$200 + 300 = 500$

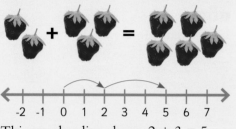

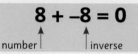

This number line shows 2 + 3 = 5.

addend The number being added.

$$2 + 6 = 8$$

addend↑   ↑addend

additive inverse When we add a number and its inverse (opposite), the answer is always zero.

$$8 + –8 = 0$$

number↑   ↑inverse

identity property of zero When zero is added to a number, the total (sum) is the same as the number.

$$4 + 0 = 4$$

repeated addition Adding the same number to itself a number of times.

$$3 + 3 + 3 + 3 = 12$$
$$5 + 5 + 5 = 15$$
$$7 + 7 + 7 = 21$$

Multiplication is a quick way of doing repeated addition:
3 + 3 + 3 + 3 is the same as 3 × 4.

See **inverse, multiplication, sum, zero**

adjacent
Next to each other, having a common point or side.

My room is adjacent to your bathroom.

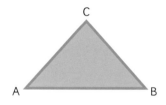

Side AB is adjacent to side AC.

algebra
An area of mathematics that uses letters and symbols to represent numbers and quantities.

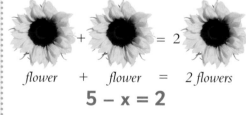

flower   +   flower   =   2 flowers

$$5 – x = 2$$

algebraic expression A calculation that contains at least one number and one unknown number (variable), but no equal sign.

verbal expression Using words to explain an algebraic expression.
See **numeral, pronumeral, variable**

algorithm

A set of rules or a method that you use to solve a problem.

Example Use blocks to find how many 3 × 4 is.

Step 1: Lay down one set of four blocks.

Step 2: Now put down the second and third sets of four.

Step 3: Exchange 10 units for one 10 (long).

Step 4: Write down your answer.
3 × 4 = 12
See **base 10 blocks**

align

Lay or place in a straight line.

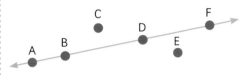

A, B, D, and F are aligned, but C and E are not.
See **line**

altitude

Height. How high something is above the Earth or sea. The altitude of this airplane is 6,500 feet (2,000 m).
See **height, surface**

6,500 ft

a.m. (ante meridiem)

See **time**

angle

The amount of turn around a fixed point (vertex). Angles are measured in degrees (°).

angle

vertex

alternate angles The two equal but opposite angles on a "Z" shape.
angle name Letters are often used to represent angles.

angle sum The angles in a polygon (flat shape) added together. The angle sum of any triangle is 180°.

a° + b° + c° = 180°

The angle sum of any quadrilateral is 360°.

a° + b° + c° + d° = 360°

amount

The total of a number of things or how much you have of a thing.
Example This is the amount of money in my change purse.

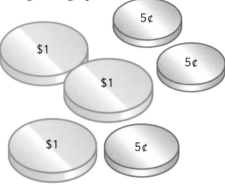

analog clock

A clock or watch with the numbers 1 to12 on its face, and two hands pointing at them to show the time.
See **digital clock**

annual

1. Happening only once a year.
Example Annual flower show.
2. Recurring yearly.
Example The annual rate of interest is 6%.
See **interest, percent**

annually A term that means "each year."

anticlockwise

Turning the opposite way from the hands of a clock.
An alternate term for counterclockwise that is used in the UK and some other countries. Screws are loosened anticlockwise.
Example
If a clock is 10 minutes fast, the hands must be moved anticlockwise 10 minutes.
See **clockwise, counterclockwise**

arm of an angle

One of the lines that makes an angle.

complementary angles Two angles that together measure 90°.

corresponding

angles Equal angles created when two parallel lines are crossed by a straight line.

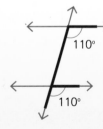

See **acute, degree, obtuse angle, parallel lines, reflex angle, right angle, straight angle, vertex**

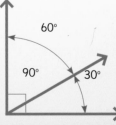

a
b
c
d
e
f
g
h
i
j
k
l
m
n
o
p
q
r
s
t
u
v
w
x
y
z

apex

Plural apexes
The top; the
highest point;
the point farthest
from the base.
It is also called
the vertex.
See **base, vertex**

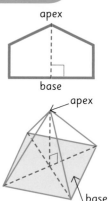

approximation

approximating, approximately
Symbols $\approx \doteq \simeq$
A result that is nearly but
not exactly the answer.
One way to approximate is to
calculate with rounded figures.
Examples
$0.9 \approx 1$
$798 \times 2.1 \approx 800 \times 2 \approx 1{,}600$
See **accurate, rounding**

arbitrary unit

Something we use to help us measure.
Handspan, pace, and objects such as
counters, bottle tops, and apples are
all arbitrary units.
Example

The area of this rectangle is
16 apples.

See **handspan, pace**

arc

A part of any curve.
See **circle, curve**

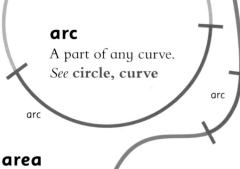

area

Symbol A
The size of, or amount of a surface.
Area is measured in square units
such as square inches (in²).

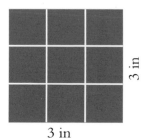

3 in (base) × 3 in (height) = 9 in²
See **conservation of area,
formula, surface, unit of
measurement**

arithmetic

The part of mathematics that deals
with numbers. We use arithmetic
for calculations with decimals, whole
numbers, and fractions.
This includes addition, subtraction,
multiplication, and division.
It is also used for measurement,
solving word problems, and working
with money.
See **computation**

array

Arrangement of objects or numbers in columns or rows.

$$\begin{array}{cccc} 3 & 7 & 12 & 5 \\ 4 & 11 & 6 & 9 \end{array}$$ an array of numbers

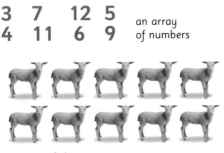

an array of sheep

arrow diagram

A diagram using arrows to show a connection between two things.
Examples
1. The connection between a set of numbers.

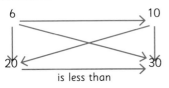

is less than

2. The connection or relationship between two sets.

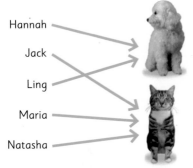

Hannah
Jack
Ling
Maria
Natasha

Children and their favorite pets.

many-to-one correspondence

This is when several items in the first set are associated with one item in the second set.
See **mapping, one-to-one correspondence, relation, set**

ascending order

Going upward or increasing in value.
See **increase, order, pattern, sequence**

askew

Not straight. At an angle.

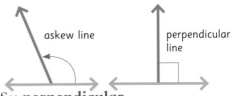

askew line

perpendicular line

See **perpendicular**

associative property

When adding or multiplying three or more numbers together, it doesn't matter how you group the numbers, the answer is the same.
Examples
Addition: $3 + 7 + 9 = 19$
so $(3 + 7) + 9 = 19$
or $3 + (7 + 9) = 19$

Multiplication: $3 \times 7 \times 9 = 189$
so $(3 \times 7) \times 9 = 189$
or $3 \times (7 \times 9) = 189$
See **commutative property**

asymmetry

Having parts that are not equal (symmetrical) in some way. An object that has no line of symmetry is described as asymmetrical.

asymmetrical

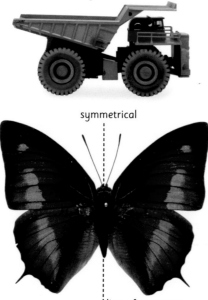

symmetrical

line of symmetry

See **line of symmetry, symmetry**

attribute

A characteristic of an object, such as size, shape, or color.
See **classification, property**

average

One score that represents a whole collection of scores. It is found by adding all the scores together and dividing the answer (sum) by the number of scores.

Example Find the average of scores 2, 5, 4, 6, and 3.

$$\text{average} = \frac{\text{sum of scores}}{\text{number of scores}}$$

$$= \frac{2 + 5 + 4 + 6 + 3}{5}$$

$$= \frac{20}{5}$$

average = 4

This is also called the mean or arithmetic mean.
See **mean, score, sum**

axis

Plural axes

1. The lines that make a graph's framework.

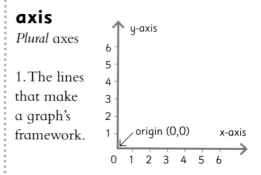

2. A line going through the center of a figure or solid. When the parts on either side of the axis look the same, it is also called an axis of symmetry.

axis

See **coordinates, graph, line of symmetry, origin**

Bb

balance

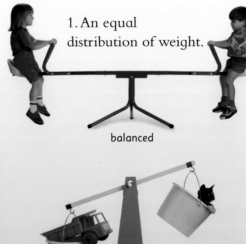

1. An equal distribution of weight.

balanced

unbalanced

2. Balance scales are a kind of scale used to weigh things.

3. The amount of money in a bank account.

You have a bank account containing.....$50.00

You take out ....$10.00 to buy a toy

Your balance is now....$40.00

bar graph

See **graph**

base

The face on which a shape or a solid stands.

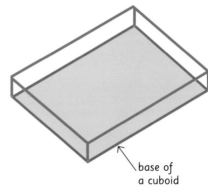

base of a cuboid

base line

1. The horizontal axis of a graph is called the base line.

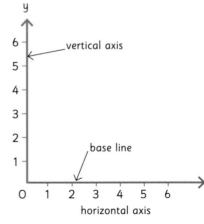

2. A base from which the heights of objects may be compared.
See **axis, horizontal line, vertical**

a
b
c
d
e
f
g
h
i
j
k
l
m
n
o
p
q
r
s
t
u
v
w
x
y
z

base 10 blocks

A set of wooden or plastic blocks used to represent a number. The most commonly used are the base 10 blocks.

A set of base 10 blocks consists of:

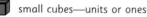 small cubes—units or ones

longs—10 small cubes joined together

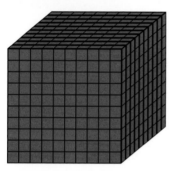
flats or squares—
100 small cubes
formed into a square

large cubes—1,000 small cubes
formed into a large cube

base 10 number system

Our number system uses 10 digits (0, 1, 2, 3, 4, 5, 6, 7, 8, 9) to make all our numbers. This is called the base 10 system.

basic facts

Operations (adding, subtracting, multiplying, and dividing) performed with one digit numbers: 0, 1, 2, 3, 4, 5, 6, 7, 8, and 9.

Addition

$0 + 0 = 0$ $0 + 1 = 1$
$1 + 1 = 2$ $9 + 9 = 18$

Multiplication

$0 \times 0 = 0$ $0 \times 1 = 0$
$1 \times 1 = 1$ $9 \times 9 = 81$

See **digit, operation, zero**

beam balance

Any balance where a beam is used.

A beam balance is used to measure the mass of an object by balancing it with an object whose mass is known.

See **balance, mass**

bi

A prefix added to the front of words and meaning two or twice.

A **bi**centennial is the 200th aniversary of an event.

A **bi**cycle has two wheels.

See **bisect**

billion

In English-speaking countries, a billion means a thousand million. It is written like this:

1,000,000,000

In much of Europe, a billion means a million million.

1,000,000,000,000

binary

A base-2 number system uses only two digits—0 and 1—to represent numbers. All numbers can be represented in a binary system. Computer systems are often written using binary codes.

bisect

To cut or divide something into two equal parts.

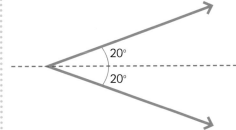

This angle has been bisected.

boundary

A line around the edge of a region. The boundary of this hexagon is its perimeter.
See **perimeter, region**

boundary

brackets

The signs ( ) [ ] { } are used for grouping numbers. In a calculation, first work out the numbers in parentheses, then in square brackets.

$2 \times [25 - (2 + 3)] = ?$

$2 + 3 = 5$

$25 - 5 = 20$

$20 \times 2 = 40$

See **order of operations, parentheses**

breadth

Another word for "width," the measurement of something from side to side.
See **width**

a
b
c
d
e
f
g
h
i
j
k
l
m
n
o
p
q
r
s
t
u
v
w
x
y
z

Cc

calculate
To work out the answer.

calorie
Symbol kcal, cal
A term for measuring
the energy of food,
also known as kilocalorie. It is the
amount of energy needed to heat
1 kg of water by 1°C. A medium-sized
(160 g) orange contains 59 kcal.

canceling
Changing a fraction to its simplest
form. The value of the fraction stays
the same, but having smaller numbers
makes it easier to work with.

$$\frac{6}{12} = \frac{3}{6} = \frac{1}{2}$$

Canceling is done by dividing the
numerator and denominator by the
same number.

numerator $\dfrac{15}{21} \dfrac{\div 3}{\div 3} = \dfrac{\cancel{15}\,^5}{\cancel{21}\,_7} = \dfrac{5}{7}$ denominator

See **denominator, factors,**
fraction, numerator

capacity
How much a container
can hold. Capacity is
measured in cubic units,
such as cubic inches.

The capacity of the
big carton of milk is
57.75 cubic inches.

The amount
(volume) of milk
in a full carton is
1 quart.

1 quart

½ quart

The capacity of the
carton will stay the same
even when some of the milk is poured out.

See **cubic unit, volume**

cardinal number
The number of all elements (items)
in a set. When we count,
we give each element a
number, starting with 1.
These numbers are
in sequence. The
last number
given is the set's
cardinal number.

Example
How many
balloons?
The cardinal
number of this set
of balloons is 4.
See **counting,**
sequence, set

Carroll diagram

See **diagram**

carrying

In arithmetic, taking a number over to the next column when the numbers in one column come to more than nine.

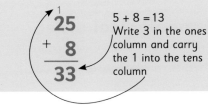

$$
\begin{array}{r}
\overset{1}{2}5 \\
+ \ \ 8 \\
\hline
33
\end{array}
$$

5 + 8 = 13
Write 3 in the ones column and carry the 1 into the tens column

See **regroup, tens, unit**

Celsius

Symbol °C
A scale used for measuring temperature. Water freezes at 0°C and boils at 100°C. Also known as centigrade.

Water boils at 100°C.

See **temperature, thermometer**

cent

Symbol ¢
A unit of money in the United States. One cent is one hundredth of a dollar.
1¢ = $0.01 $1 = 100¢
See **dollar**

center

A point in the middle of something that is the same distance from all outer points.
See **circle, radius**

centi

A prefix meaning one hundredth. One centimeter is a hundredth of a meter.
1 cm = 0.01 m

Each small line on this scale represents 1 cg.

centigram *Symbol* cg
A metric unit of mass.
100 cg = 1 kilogram
centiliter *Symbol* cl
A metric unit of capacity.
100 cl = 1 liter
centimeter *Symbol* cm
A metric unit of length.
100 cm = 1 meter
See **capacity, decimal, metric system, unit of measurement**

century

One hundred.
100 years, 100 points in a game, etc. From January 1, 1901, to December 31, 2000, is the 20th century. The 21st century began on January 1, 2001.

certain

A 100% chance of an event happening.
See **chance, event, probability**

chance

A likelihood of an event happening.
See **event, probability**

checking

A way of making sure that an answer is correct. One way of checking is by using an inverse (opposite) calculation.

1. Addition is checked by subtraction.

$$15 + 28 = 43$$
$$43 - 28 = 15$$

The answer 43 is correct.

2. Division is checked by multiplication.

$$20 \div 4 = 5$$
$$5 \times 4 = 20$$

The answer 5 is correct.
See **inverse**

chronological order

The arrangement of events by when they happened, with the earliest coming first.

09:00 a.m.	Homeroom
09:30 a.m.	English
11:00 a.m.	Math
12:30 a.m.	Lunch

The timetable is in chronological order.
See **time**

circle

A 2-D shape that has a curved edge, with each part of the curve the same distance away from the shape's center.

chord A line that joins two points on a circle's edge. The diameter is the longest chord in a circle and always goes through the circle's center.

circle graph Another name for a pie chart.

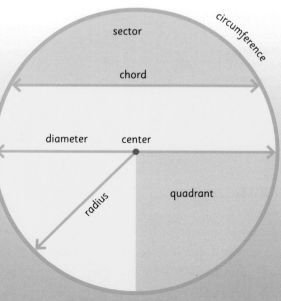

circle

A round 2-D shape (see box below).

class

A group, set, or collection of things. Triangles, squares, rectangles, and kites belong to the class of polygons.

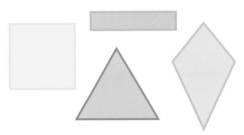

classification

Organization into classes, sets, or groups, according to attributes.
See **attribute, property, sorting**

clockwise

The direction in which the hands of a clock normally travel. Screws and bottle tops are tightened clockwise.

A clock's hands move in a clockwise direction.
See **anticlockwise, counterclockwise**

circular In the form of a circle; round. Something in the form of half a circle is semicircular.

A protractor is semicircular.

circumference The edge, or perimeter, of a circle. The distance around a circle.

See **center, diameter, graph, perimeter, pi, plane, quadrant, radius, sector**

A dart board is circular.

a b c d e f g h i j k l m n o p q r s t u v w x y z

closed figure

A 2-D shape
(polygon) with sides
that begin and end
at the same point.
See **polygon,
shape**

closed figures

code

A system of words, letters, or symbols
that represents other letters, words, or
sentences. Codes are used for secret
writing or signaling.

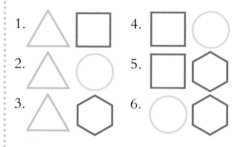

This is "mother" in Morse code.

coefficient

The number in front of a variable
in an algebraic term.

3y   3 is the coefficient of y.
See **algebra, variable**

column

A vertical arrangement.

13
5
18
27
9
31

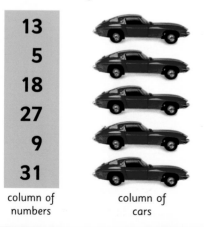

column of   column of
numbers   cars

combination

A way of grouping objects together.
There are four shapes in this group:

Possible pairings include:

1. △ □   4. □ ○

2. △ ○   5. □ ⬡

3. △ ⬡   6. ○ ⬡

Each pairing is a combination.
The order in which the shapes
are placed is not important.
See **permutation, set, subset**

combined shapes

2-D shapes that are
made of two or
more polygons.
They are also known
as complex shapes.

To calculate the
area of a combined shape.
1. First divide it into simple shapes.
2. Find the area of each shape.
3. Add the areas to find the total.

$A_1 + A_2 =$ Total area

See **area**

common denominator

A number that all the denominators for two or more fractions divide into exactly.

Example
The denominators for one-half (2) and one-third (3) divide exactly into 6, 12, 18, etc. So 6, 12, and 18, etc. are their common denominators.
See **denominator, fraction, lowest common denominator**

commutative property

We can add or multiply two or more numbers in any order and the answer will be the same.

$$6 + 4 = 10$$
$$4 + 6 = 10$$

$$3 \times 8 = 24$$
$$8 \times 3 = 24$$

See **associative property**

comparison

Looking at objects, measures, or quantities to see how they are the same and how they are different.
See **division, ratio**

needle

compass

An instrument that shows direction. It is marked with the directions north (N), east (E), south (S), and west (W). A compass contains a magnet that makes the needle point toward the Earth's Magnetic North Pole. All other directions can be found by lining up the needle with N.
See **direction**

same heights   different heights

a b c d e f g h i j k l m n o p q r s t u v w x y z

compasses

An instrument
that is designed
for drawing a
circle and
marking off
equal lengths.
Also known as
a pair of
compasses

The compass
point sits in
the center of
the circle.

compatible numbers

Numbers that make it easier to
estimate the answer to multiplication
or division problems because they are
easy to multiply or divide.

To estimate 42 × 9, round down
42 to 40 and round up 9 to 10.
40 × 10 is 400.
See **estimate, rounding**

complement

Something that completes or fills
up a whole.
See **angles, complementary
addition**

complementary addition

1. Finding the amount needed to
complete a set. *Example* What has
to be added to seven to make ten?

$$7 + ? = 10$$

Three has to be added.

2. Counting on to a higher total.
Example

My shopping costs $17.50.
I pay with a $20 bill.
How much change should I get?
My change is worked out by
counting on to find what must
be added to $17.50 to get $20.
I get $2.50 change.

$$\$17.50 + ? = \$20$$

3. The method of "subtracting" that
changes the subtraction question to
an addition question.
Example

$$? - 19 = 2$$

could be viewed as:

$$19 + 2 = ?$$

The answer is 21.
See **addition, subtraction**

composite number

A number with factors other than itself and 1. Factors are whole numbers that divide exactly into another number.

$$12 = 12 \times 1$$
$$\text{or } 3 \times 4$$
$$\text{or } 6 \times 2$$
$$\text{or } 3 \times 2 \times 2$$

Twelve is a composite number. Every whole number greater than 1 is either a composite number (4, 6, 8, 9, 10, 12, 14…), or a prime number (2, 3, 5, 7, 11…).
See **factors, prime number**

compound operation

See **order of operations**

computation

compute, computing
Using addition, subtraction, multiplication, and/or division to calculate (work out) the answer to a mathematical question. These operations can be done mentally, in writing, or with the help of calculating aids such as an abacus, tables, calculators, and computers.
See **abacus, operation, table**

concave

A shape that is rounded inward or hollowed like the inside of a bowl.

concave

See **convex**

concentric circles

Two or more circles that have the same center.
See **circle**

× center

cone

A solid with a circular base, coming to a point at the top, similar to an ice-cream cone.
See **solid, three-dimensional**

congruent

Symbol $\cong$

Matching exactly in size and shape.

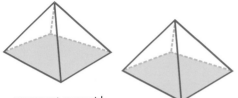

congruent pyramids

congruent triangles Two or more triangles with the same-sized sides and angles.
See **triangle**

corresponding sides A matching pair of sides in a shape.
See **similar**

conjecture

A guess based on information that is complete.

consecutive numbers

Numbers that follow each other in a sequence.

1 2 3 4 5 6 7 8

See **sequence**

conservation of area

Keeping the same area, even though the shapes are different.
These three shapes have the same area of 3 sq in.
See **area**

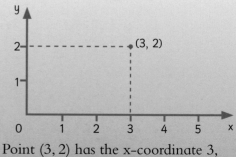

coordinates

A set of numbers or letters that shows the position of something. You use a pair of coordinates to find the position of a point on a flat (plane) surface, such as a map. The first number is the x-coordinate (how far across something is), the second is the y-coordinate (how far up something is).
One way to remember which comes first is to say "along the corridor and up the stairs."

1. Coordinates can be plotted on a coordinate plane—a chart with an x-axis and a y-axis. The coordinates are written in parentheses.

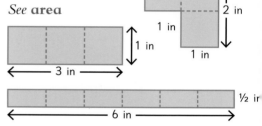

Point (3, 2) has the x-coordinate 3, and the y-coordinate 2.

constant

A number that always has the same value. The opposite of variable.

$$2c + 6$$ 6 is the constant.

continuous data

Information (data) consisting of measurements that can be made on a continuous scale, such as temperature, mass, or distance.

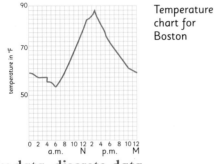

Temperature chart for Boston

See **data, discrete data**

converging lines

Two or more lines that meet at the same point.

P

See **perspective**

convex

Shaped like the outside of a circle or a sphere. The opposite of concave.

convex

The cycle helmet has a **convex** top.

See **concave**

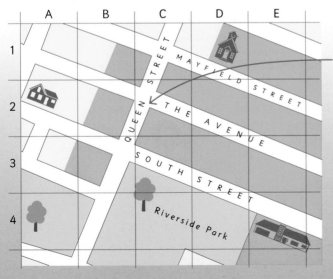

2. The position of the junction for The Avenue and Queen Street is C2.

My house is at A2. My Grandma's house is at D1. My school is at E4.

See **axis, graph, intersection, ordered pair, origin**

a
b
c
d
e
f
g
h
i
j
k
l
m
n
o
p
q
r
s
t
u
v
w
x
y
z

correspondence

See **arrow diagram,**
one–to–one correspondence

corresponding sides

See **congruent**

counterclockwise

Turning the opposite way from
the hands of a clock. Screws
and bottle tops are loosened
by turning them in a
counterclockwise direction.
See **anticlockwise, clockwise**

counting

Giving one number to
every item in a set.
The numbers
are in sequence.

1

2

3

4

5

counting number

All the positive
whole numbers
used in counting:

{1, 2, 3, 4 … }.

Zero is not a counting number.
counting system A way of finding
out how many objects there are.
See **cardinal number, decimal,**
sequence, set

counting principle

Multiplying the number of ways
something can occur in order to find
the number of possible outcomes.

Example
The café serves two types of pizza.
You can choose one of four toppings.

cheese pizza

meat pizza

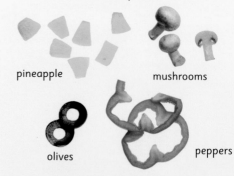

pineapple

mushrooms

olives

peppers

For each type of pizza, there are five
options: one of four toppings, or no
topping at all. Therefore, there are 10
(2 pizzas × 5 options) options in total.

cube

A solid shaped like a box with 12 equal edges, six equal square faces, and eight corners (vertices).

A cube is a type of cuboid.

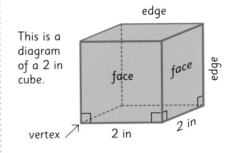

This is a diagram of a 2 in cube.

edge

face   face

edge

vertex   2 in   2 in

This cube puzzle is made up of 27 smaller cubes.

See **cuboid, face, hexahedron, solid**

credit

1. A payment of money.
Example
His bank account showed last month's credits.
2. An agreement that payment will be made at a later date for money, goods, or services.
Example
He bought a bed on credit.
See **debit**

cross-section of a solid

A cut through a solid from one side to the other; a slice of an object.

Cross-section of a lemon

See **face, front view, plan, plane, section, side view**

cubed number

When a number is cubed, it is multiplied by itself three times.

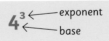

4^3 ← exponent
← base

4^3 means $4 \times 4 \times 4$ or 64.
We read it as "4 cubed," "4 cube," or "4 to the third power."
See **exponent, power of a number, square number**

cubic unit

The way volume is measured.

cubic centimeter A unit used for measuring volume.

1 cm³ has a capacity of 1 milliliter.

cubic meter A unit used for measuring volume.

$1 m^3 = 1,000,000 cm^3$

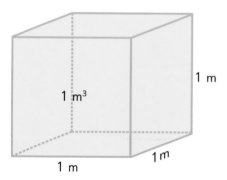

A cube with edges that are 1 meter long has a volume of 1 cubic meter. 1 m³ has a capacity of 1 kiloliter.

See **capacity, cube, unit of measurement, volume**

cup

Symbol c

A measurement of capacity used in cooking. The capacity of one cup is equivalent to half a pint (8 ounces).

Example Add one cup of flour.

See **capacity**

curve

A line with no straight parts. There are open curves and closed curves.

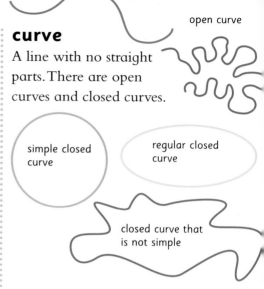

open curve

simple closed curve

regular closed curve

closed curve that is not simple

See **circle, ellipse**

customary measurement system

The main measurement system in the United States. It originated in the United Kingdom and is called the Imperial measurement system. Measurements include pint, ounce, and pound, among others.

cylinder

A shape like a can. It is a solid with two circular faces at right angles to a curved surface.

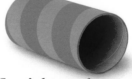

See **right angle**

Dd

data

A collection of facts, numbers, measurements, or symbols.

Example

Students' scores on a math test.

Jack	15
Eduardo	16
Jasmine	18
Isabelle	19
Joe	20

debit

An amount of money taken out of an account.

See **credit**

deca (deka)

Prefix that means 10.

decameter (dekameter) A metric unit of length equal to 10 meters.

decaliter (dekaliter) A metric unit of volume equal to 10 liters.

decagram (dekagram) A metric unit of weight equal to 10 grams.

See **decagon, decahedron**

decade

Ten years.

decagon

A 2-D shape (polygon) with 10 sides.

regular decagon

irregular decagon

decahedron

A 3-D shape (polyhedron) with 10 faces.

Example

This decahedron has been made by joining two pyramids and cutting off their tops.

See **polyhedron**

deci

A prefix meaning one-tenth.

decigram A metric unit that measures weight. It is equal to one-tenth of a kilogram.

deciliter A metric unit that measures capacity. It is equal to one-tenth of a liter, or 100 milliliters.

decimeter A metric unit that measures length. It is equal to one-tenth of a meter or 10 centimeters.

decimal

Containing 10 parts.
decimal number A fraction written as a decimal.

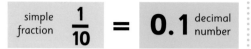

| simple fraction | $\dfrac{1}{10}$ | = | **0.1** | decimal number |

decimal place-value system
A system of numbers that is based on groups of ten. Also called the "base ten" system, or the decimal system. The position of the digit shows the value of the number.
1,000 is 10^3 and has 3 zeros after the 1.
0.01 is 10^{-2} and has 3 zeros before the 1.

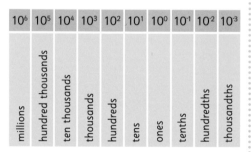

10^6	10^5	10^4	10^3	10^2	10^1	10^0	10^{-1}	10^{-2}	10^{-3}
millions	hundred thousands	ten thousands	thousands	hundreds	tens	ones	tenths	hundredths	thousandths

decimal point A point, period, or dot that separates a whole number from a part of a number (a decimal number). A comma is used instead of a point in many other parts of the world.

32.4
decimal point
7,62

See **place value, point**

decrease

To make smaller or reduce.
To decrease something, you must either subtract a number from it or divide it by a number.

Example

The number of bottles was decreased from 3 to 2 by subtracting 1.
See **increase**

deduct

To take away. Another word for subtract.
See **subtraction**

degree

Symbol °
In geometry, a degree is a unit used for measuring angles.

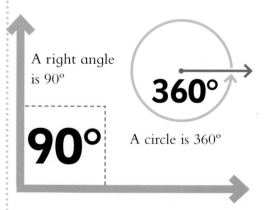

A right angle is 90°

360°
A circle is 360°

90°

See **angle, Celsius**

denominator

The number written below the line in a fraction. It tells how many parts there are in the whole.

Example

This circle has been divided into 6 equal parts.

$\frac{5}{6}$ ← numerator
  ← denominator

In $\frac{5}{6}$ the denominator is 6.

like denominators Denominators that match; a common denominator.

$$\frac{1}{8} + \frac{3}{8}$$

unlike denominators
Denominators that do not match.

$$\frac{1}{2} + \frac{3}{5}$$

See **fraction, lowest common denominator, numerator**

depth

How deep something is. Depth is measured from the top down, from the front to the back, or from the surface inward.

depth of box

descending order

Going down or decreasing in value.

Example

The following lengths have been arranged in descending order:

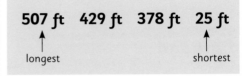

507 ft   429 ft   378 ft   25 ft

↑ longest   ↑ shortest

diagonal

1. Something that is slanting.
2. A slanting line joining two corners that are not next to each other in a shape.

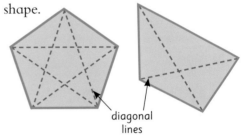

diagonal lines

diagram

A picture that shows information.

Example A Carroll diagram shows how things are sorted into groups.

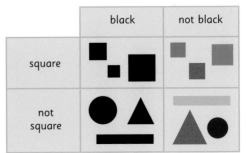

	black	not black
square		
not square		

a b c **d** e f g h i j k l m n o p q r s t u v w x y z

diameter

A straight line that passes through the center of a circle and reaches from one side to the other.

See **circle, line, radius**

diameter

center

diamond

A 2-D shape with four equal sides and four angles that are not right angles. The correct name is rhombus.

70°

110°

See **dimension, rhombus**

die

Plural dice

A regular 3-D shape, usually a cube, marked with spots or numerals.

One die   Two dice

Some dice have more than six faces.

difference

The amount one quantity (such as a number or a dimension) is bigger or smaller than another. You find the difference by subtracting the smaller number from the bigger.

Example

$$10 - 3 = 7$$

The difference between 10 and 3 is 7.

dimension

A measure of size including length, width, and height.

1. One-dimensional (1-D) objects have only length.

Examples lines, curves

line

curve

2. Two-dimensional (2-D) objects have length and width.

Examples polygons, circles

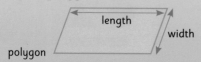

length

width

polygon

3. Three-dimensional (3-D) objects have length, width, and height.

Examples cubes, pyramids

height

length

width

A point (dot) has no dimensions.

See **one-dimensional, plane, space, three-dimensional, two-dimensional**

digit

Numerals 0 to 9 are called digits.
They are used to make other numbers.
Examples

56 is a two-digit number.

813 is a three-digit number.

See **place value**

digital clock

A clock or a watch that shows time
by numbers. It has no clock hands.
Example
This clock shows
10 to 10.
See **analog
clock, time**

dimension

A measure of size (see box, left).

direction

1. The way to go.
Left, right, up, down, above, below,
inside, outside, near, forward,
backward, etc.
2. Compass directions:
north (N), east (E),
south (S), west (W),
northeast (NE),
southeast (SE),
southwest (SW),
northwest (NW).

See **clockwise,
compass,
counterclockwise**

direct proportion

See **proportion**

discount

If the price of something is
reduced, it is sold at a discount.
Discounts are often offered as
a percentage of the selling price.

discrete data

A set of data that is based on counting.
It deals in whole numbers (things that
cannot be broken into smaller bits,
such as goals—you can't have half
a goal).

Number of goals
scored last season

See **continuous data, data**

displacement

A change in the position of an object or of a quantity of material.
Example Dropping a die into water displaces some water.

The volume of displaced water is equal to the volume of the die.

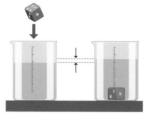

See **volume**

distance

The length between two points.

distribute

Give a share of something to each.
Example Mom will distribute the cupcakes.

division

Splitting a quantity into smaller, equal groups. This can be done in different ways:
1. Grouping (quotition).
Example

How many groups of 3 can be made with 15 apples?
The apples are to be placed into groups of equal size, 3 to a group.

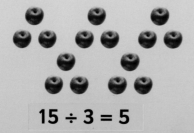

$$15 \div 3 = 5$$

There are 5 groups of 3 apples.

2. Sharing (partition).
Example
Share 15 apples among 5 children. How many apples will each child get? The apples are to be separated into 5 equal groups.

$$15 \div 5 = 3$$

Each child will get 3 apples.

3. Ratio (comparing quantities).
The ratio of squash to water is 1:5 (1 part squash to 5 parts water).

20 oz   to   100 oz

How much squash will you need for 100 oz of water? You divide 100 by 5 to find out. 100 ÷ 5 = 20. You will need 20oz of squash.

See **ratio**

distribution

See **frequency distribution**

distributive property

When you multiply a number by a two-digit number, this is the same as multiplying by each digit separately.

$$3 \times 24$$
$$= (3 \times 20) + (3 \times 4)$$
$$= 60 + 12 = 72$$

dividend

1. A number that is to be divided by another number.

$$24 \div 6 = 4$$

dividend ↑   ↑   ↑ quotient
      divisor

24 is the dividend.

2. What you receive as interest on money you have invested.

See **division, interest, quotient**

divisible

A number is divisible by another number if, after dividing, there is no remainder.

$$72 \div 9 = 8$$

72 is divisible by 9 and also by 8.

Note No number can be divided by 0.

divisor

A number that is to be divided into another number.

$$24 \div 6 = 4$$

dividend │   │   │ quotient
      divisor

6 is the divisor.

See **dividend, factors, quotient, ratio, remainder**

divisibility tests

A number is divisible by...	if...	Examples
2	the last digit is even	2, 4, 6, 122, 358, 1,000
3	the sum of all digits can be divided by 3	261: $2+6+1=9$ 18: $1+8=9$
4	the last two digits are divisible by 4	124: $24 \div 4 = 6$
5	the last digit is 5 or 0	15, 70
6	the last digit is even and the sum of its digits is divisible by 3	7,446: $7+4+4+6=21$
7	there is no divisibility test	
8	the last 3 digits are divisible by 8	5,384: $384 \div 8 = 48$
9	the sum of its digits is divisible by 9	3,123: $3+1+2+3=9$
10	the number ends in 0	10, 20, 30...

dodecagon

A 2-D shape (polygon) with 12 sides.

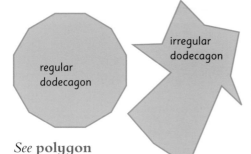

regular dodecagon

irregular dodecagon

See **polygon**

dodecahedron

A solid 3-D shape (polyhedron) with 12 faces. A regular dodecahedron is made by joining together 12 regular pentagons.

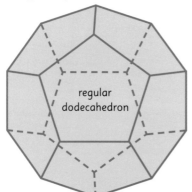

regular dodecahedron

See **pentagon, polyhedron**

dollar

Symbol $

A unit of money used in the United States, Canada, Australia, and New Zealand, divided into 100 cents.

See **cent**

dot paper

Paper printed with dots arranged in a pattern. It is used for drawing shapes, playing games, and to record work done on a geo-board.

Examples

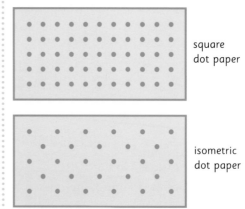

square dot paper

isometric dot paper

See **geo-board, square paper**

double

Twice as many, or the same again.

double 8 is 16

10 is double 5

dozen

Twelve items.

One dozen eggs = 12 eggs.

Ee

edge

Where two sides
(faces) meet
on a shape.

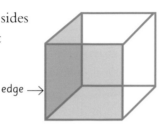

edge →

See **face, intersection, plane**

element of a set

One of the objects within a set.

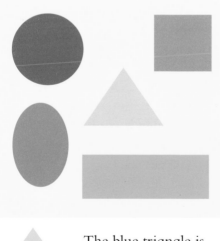

The blue triangle is
an element of the
set of shapes above.

See **cardinal number, set**

ellipse

A curved shape
that looks like
a stretched-
out circle.
Example
A football
is elliptical.
See **curve**

enlarge

To make something bigger.
This can be done using devices such
as a photocopier, grid, or projector.
Enlargement is a common type of
transformation.

projector

picture
of a dog

enlarged image

A projector uses light rays
to enlarge a picture.
See **reduce, scale drawing,
transformation**

equal

Symbol =

1. Identical in amount or quantity.
Example These two bags of sugar
are of equal weight.

2. Of the same value.

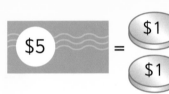

$5 bill = five $1 coins

3. Sums that express the same thing
in different ways.

$$1 + 8 = \quad 3 + 6 =$$
$$5 + 4 = \quad 2 + 7 =$$

These sums are equal because they
all represent the number 9.

equal sign The name
of the symbol that means
"is equal to" or "equals."
It looks like this:

=

equalizer A beam balance with
numbered hooks on which number
facts balance when they are equal.
See **balance, equality**

equality

Being equal. Having the same value,
as shown by an equal sign.

$$2 + 4 = 6$$

See **equal, equation, inequality**

equally likely

See **event, probability**

equation

A statement that says that two
amounts (quantities) are equal.
An equation has two balanced sides
joined by an equal sign.

This equation is true only if x has
the value of three:

$$x + 4 = 7$$

See **equality, inequality,
place holder, variable**

equilateral

Having sides of equal length.
Regular polygons have angles of
equal size and sides of equal length.

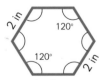

regular hexagon

regular square

equilateral triangle

A triangle that has three sides of equal length and three equal angles.
The angles of any equilateral triangle are always 60°.
See **triangle**

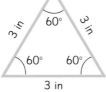

equivalent

Having the same value or amount. A $1 coin is equivalent to two 50¢ coins.

estimate

1. A rough or approximate calculation; a number that has not been calculated accurately.
Estimated answers are often needed when working with decimals.
19.8 × 3 can be estimated as 20 × 3, so 19.8 × 3 = 60.
See **approximation, calculate, rounding**

Euro

Symbol €
A currency used in many countries throughout Europe. It is divided into 100 cents.

evaluate

To find the value of.
The value of 21 × 3 is 63.

even

Equally balanced, equal in number or amount.

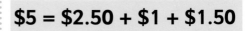

$$\$5 = \$2.50 + \$1 + \$1.50$$

even number

A number that is divisible by two. All even numbers finish with one of these digits:

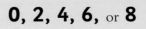

0, 2, 4, 6, or **8**

See **digit, division**

event

A term used in probability. Something that can happen as a result of performing an experiment.
Example
The experiment is rolling one die. Many events are possible: rolling a 3; getting an even number; getting an odd number, etc.

compound event An event that involves the use of at least two items, such as rolling two dice.
dependent event An event where the outcome of one event affects the outcome of another.
Example
If you wake up late, you will miss the bus.
See **outcome, probability**

exact

Precise, accurate, correct in every way, not approximate.

See **approximation**

exchange

To give something and receive something else in return.

1. When we go shopping, we exchange money for goods.
2. Coins and bills can be exchanged for different coins and bills of the same value.

25¢ can be exchanged for two 10¢ coins and one 5¢ coin.

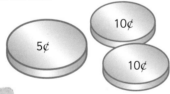

exchange rate

The comparison of values of money between different countries.

$1.00 = £0.70

$1.00 = €0.76

See **comparison, equivalent**

expand

Write out in full.

1. Expand 4

2. Expand 537

537 = 500 + 30 + 7

expanded notation

A way of writing numerals or algebraic expressions.

249 = 200 + 40 + 9

or

(2 × 100) + (4 × 10) + (9 × 1)

exponent

A number that shows how many times a quantity is to be multiplied by itself.

See **index, power of a number**

exterior

The outside of something.

exterior   interior

Ff

face

In a 3-D shape, a face is the flat part of the surface that is bounded by the edges.

1. A cube has six faces.

2. A triangle-based pyramid (tetrahedron) has four faces.

3. A square-based pyramid has five faces.

See **cube, edge, pyramid, tetrahedron, three-dimensional**

factors

All the whole numbers that can be divided exactly into another number.

$$6 \div 1 = 6 \quad 1$$
$$6 \div 2 = 3 \quad 2$$
$$6 \div 3 = 2 \quad 3$$
$$6 \div 6 = 1 \quad 6$$

factor

1, 2, 3, and 6 are factors of 6.

The prime number 5 has only the factors 5 and 1.

factor

$$5 \div 1 = 5$$
$$5 \div 5 = 1$$

common factor A number that can divide both parts of a fraction exactly. It is used to help simplify a fraction.

greatest common factor
The largest whole number that can be divided by each of the numbers in a fraction.
Example $\frac{4}{8}$
4 and 8 can be divided exactly by 2 and 4, so 2 and 4 are the common factors. The greatest common factor is 4.

$$\frac{4}{8} \quad 4 \div 4 = 1$$
$$\qquad 8 \div 4 = 2$$

$\frac{4}{8}$ in its simplest form is $\frac{1}{2}$.
See **composite number, factor tree, fraction, prime number, whole numbers**

factor tree

A diagram showing prime factors—prime numbers that divide exactly into a given number.
See **prime factor**

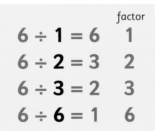

prime factors of 18

a b c d e f g h i j k l m n o p q r s t u v w x y z

Fahrenheit

A temperature scale in which water freezes at 32° and boils at 212°. To convert from Fahrenheit to Celsius, subtract 32 and divide by 1.8.

false sentence

A sentence about numbers that is not true.
The open sentence 3 + ? = 10 becomes false if it is completed by any other number than 7. If it is completed by 7, it will become a true sentence.
See **number sentence, true sentence**

farthest

The longest distance away.

Name	Distance
Paul	3.50 yd
Kate	4 yd
Mike	3.75 yd

Kate jumped the farthest.

See **distance**

figure

Another name for a numeral, line, shape, or solid.
1. Thirty-six written in figures is 36.
2. Half of this figure has been colored in.

finite

Anything that has boundaries or can be counted.
1. The region inside a square is finite because it is bounded by sides.
2. The set of months in a year is a finite set because the months can be counted.
See **infinite, perimeter, region, set**

first

The one at the beginning, before any other.

Starting from the left, the first doll is the biggest.

flat

1. Being in one plane only.

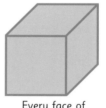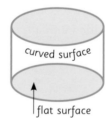

curved surface

flat surface

Every face of a cube is flat.

2. The name used for the base 10 block representing one hundred.
See **base 10 blocks, face, plane, surface**

flip

To turn over.

See **reflection, slide, turn**

This playing card has been flipped over.

flowchart

A way of describing a problem-solving rule using symbols.

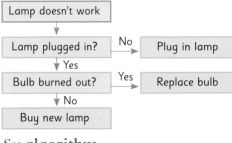

See **algorithm**

foot

Plural feet

Symbols ', ft

A measure of length.

1 foot = 12 inches

1 foot ≈ 30 centimeters

See **customary measurement system, metric system**

formula

Plural formulas, formulae

An equation that uses symbols to represent a statement.

length *l*

$$A = lw$$

width *w*

The area of a rectangle is its length (*l*) multiplied by its width (*w*).

See **area, equation**

fraction

A part of a whole quantity or number.

Examples

The fraction $\frac{1}{6}$ means 1 part out of 6 equal parts. One sixth $\left(\frac{1}{6}\right)$ of the pie is missing.

$\frac{1}{6}$

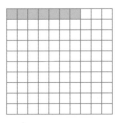

7 parts out of 100 parts are colored in. The fraction is $\frac{7}{100}$.

Show $\frac{3}{4}$ of 8.

$$\frac{6}{8} = \frac{3}{4}$$

lowest terms A fraction is in its lowest terms when the greatest common factor (the largest whole number that divides exactly into the numerator and denominator) is 1. $\frac{4}{64}$ reduced to its lowest terms is $\frac{1}{16}$.

unit fraction A fraction with a numerator and denominator that are whole numbers. Also called a common fraction.

numerator ⟶ $\dfrac{4}{5}$ ⟵ denominator

See **decimal fraction, factors, improper fraction, proper fraction**

frequency

The number of times an item occurs in a collection of data.

Example

We tossed a die 50 times and recorded the number for each throw. We kept a tally of the 50 scores.

Number	Tally	Frequency
1	⊞⊞ II	7
2	⊞⊞ ⊞⊞ II	12
3	⊞⊞ IIII	9
4	⊞⊞ III	8
5	⊞⊞ I	6
6	⊞⊞ III	8

Number 2 had the highest frequency. Number 5 had the lowest frequency.
See **data, frequency distribution, tally**

frequency distribution

A graph or table showing how often an event or quantity occurs.

Example

A frequency distribution table of grades for a math test within a class:

Grade	Tally	Frequency
20-29	I	1
30-39	⊞⊞	5
40-49	⊞⊞ IIII	9
50-59	⊞⊞ III	8
60-69	⊞⊞	5
70-79	III	3
80-89	I	1
	Total	32

frequency table

See **frequency distribution**

front view

A diagram of an object as seen from directly in front of it.

A front view of a house.

See **plan, side view**

Gg

gallon

An Imperial measure of volume.

1 gallon ≈ 4.5 liters

geo-board

A board studded with
nails that form a
pattern or grid,
usually of squares or
equilateral triangles. You put rubber
bands on the nails to make shapes.
See **equilateral triangle,
grid, pattern**

geometry

The part of mathematics that deals with
solids, surfaces, lines, angles, and space.
See **measure, solid, space, surface**

geo-strips

Strips of plastic, metal, or cardboard
with holes equally spaced down the
center of the strips. They are used
for making shapes.

shapes made
using geo-strips

googol

A very large number. It has the
numeral 1 with one hundred
zeros after it.

$$1,000,000,000,000,\\000,000,000,000...$$

graduated

Marked off with measurements.
A ruler is graduated in inches
or centimeters.

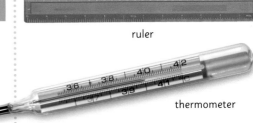

ruler

thermometer

A thermometer is
graduated in degrees.

gram

Symbol g
A unit of mass.

1,000 g = 1 kg

The mass of this box
of cereal is 250 grams.
See **mass, unit of
measurement**

a b c d e f g h i j k l m n o p q r s t u v w x y z

45

graph

A drawing or diagram that combines information about several things. There are different types of graph.

bar graph Horizontal or vertical bars used to show information. A bar graph with vertical bars or columns is also called a column graph.

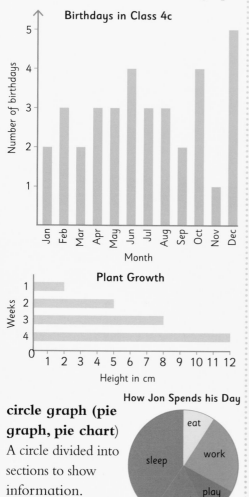

circle graph (pie graph, pie chart) A circle divided into sections to show information.

histogram A column graph with no spaces between the columns.

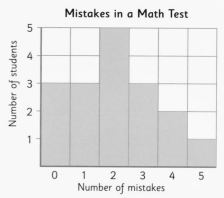

line graph A graph where you plot points then join them together to show information.

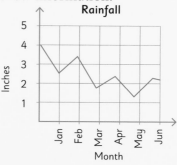

pictograph A graph where pictures represent real objects. Also known as picture graph or pictogram.

Class 7b—Favorite Fruit

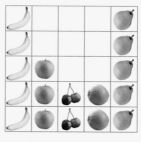

KEY: 1 picture stands for 1 person who prefers that fruit

graph paper

See **square paper**

greater than

Symbol >

More than, bigger than.
An expression that shows which
number is larger in a pair of numbers.
See **inequality, less than**

greatest common factor

See **factors**

grid

Sets of parallel lines that cross each
other at right angles. Often found
on maps and graphs.

See **parallel lines, right angle,
square paper**

gross

Twelve dozen (12 × 12); 144.

group

1. Putting things together in a set or
group. In the decimal system, things
are grouped into tens.

hundreds	tens	units
2	4	3

243 = 2 groups of 100
4 groups of 10
3 groups of 1

2. Two or more things.

a group of boys

grouping Putting things together
into sets with the same number in
each set. This is also called quotition.

How many groups of four can be
made with twenty balls?

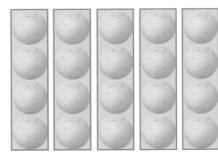

The answer is five groups of four.
See **division, set, tens, unit**

Hh

half

Plural halves
One part of two
equal parts.
1. Half of a circle.
2. Half of twenty-four
is twelve. $\frac{1}{2} \times 24 = 12$
3. This orange
has been cut
into two halves.

handspan

The distance between the thumb tip
and the smallest finger tip on an
outstretched hand.

This is a handspan.

A handspan is used as a rough
measure for estimating the lengths,
heights, or widths of objects.
See **arbitrary unit, estimate**

hecta, hecto

A prefix meaning 100 that is added
to the beginning of a word.

hectare *Symbol* ha
A metric unit of
area. One hectare
is the area of a
square with sides
of 100 meters.
The area of a
soccer field is
approximately
half a hectare.

hectogram A metric unit of
mass equal to 100 grams.
hectoliter A metric unit of
volume equal to 100 liters.
hectometer A metric unit of
length equal to 100 meters.
See **area, unit of measurement**

height

Symbol h
Measurement from top to bottom,
the vertical distance.
See **altitude, vertical**

hemisphere

Half of a sphere.
The Earth is divided
into the northern
and southern
hemispheres.

northern
hemisphere

southern
hemisphere

See **sphere**

heptagon

A 2-D shape with seven sides and seven angles. Regular heptagons have all sides and all angles the same; irregular heptagons do not.

regular heptagon   irregular heptagons

hexagon

A 2-D shape (polygon) that has six sides and six angles.

regular hexagon   irregular hexagons

Honeycomb is made up of regular hexagons.

hexagram

A shape formed by two intersecting equilateral triangles.
See **equilateral, intersect**

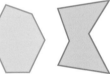

hexahedron

A hexahedron is a 3-D shape with six faces. All cuboids are hexahedrons.
See **cube, cuboid, polyhedron, prism, three-dimensional**

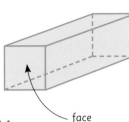

face

Hindu–Arabic

Our modern system of numbers. The symbols for all the digits, except zero, may have been developed as early as 200 BCE by the Hindus in India.

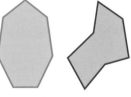

Hindu numerals

The Arabs adopted the system, and added zero.

٠	١	٢	٣	٤	٥	٦	٧	٨	٩
0	1	2	3	4	5	6	7	8	9

Arabic numerals (13th century)

0 1 2 3 4 5 6 7 8 9

Hindu-Arabic numerals

The system only has ten digits, with zero as a place holder. The numerals, including zero, were standardized after the printing press was invented in the 15th century.
See **place holder, place value**

a b c d e f g **h** i j k l m n o p q r s t u v w x y z

histogram

See graph

horizon

The line at which the land and sky appear to meet.

horizon

See **horizontal line**

horizontal line

A line that is parallel to the horizon. A vertical line is at a right angle to the horizon.

vertical line

horizontal line

See **base line, parallel lines, right angle, vertical**

horizontal plane

Any surface that is parallel to the horizon.

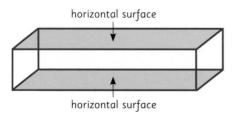

horizontal surface

horizontal surface

See **horizon, parallel lines, surface**

hour

See **time**

hundred

$100 = 10 \times 10$

hundredth

$\frac{1}{100} = 1 \div 100$

hundred thousand

$100,000 = 100 \times 1000$

hundred thousandth

$\frac{1}{100,000} = 1 \div 100,000$

See **decimal place value system**

hypotenuse

The longest side of a right-angled triangle, which is the side opposite to the right angle.

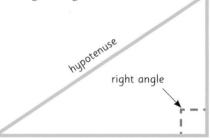

hypotenuse

right angle

Ii

icosahedron

A 3-D shape with twenty faces.
A regular icosahedron
is formed by joining
together twenty
identical
equilateral
triangles.

See **polyhedron**

identical

Exactly alike.

image

An exact copy of an object.

mirror
image

See **mapping, mirror image,
reflection**

Imperial system

Another name for the customary
measurement system.

See **customary measurement system**

improper fraction

A fraction whose numerator is greater
than its denominator.

$$\frac{12}{10}$$ ← numerator
← denominator

inch

Symbol ”, in
A measure of length.

This is
an inch.

12 inches = 1 foot

increase

Make larger by adding or multiplying.
See **decrease, progression**

index

Plural indices
Also called the exponent. It indicates
how many times a number has to
be multiplied by itself to produce
the answer.

index or
exponent

base → 10^6

could also be written as

$10 \times 10 \times 10 \times 10 \times 10 \times 10$

$= 1,000,000$

This is called ten
to the power of 6.

See **exponent,
power of a number**

a
b
c
d
e
f
g
h
i
j
k
l
m
n
o
p
q
r
s
t
u
v
w
x
y
z

indirect measuring

Also known as shadow-stick measuring. Indirect measuring is used to calculate heights that you cannot measure directly.

Example

To measure the height of a tree, use a stick 2 yd long and measure its shadow. Then measure the shadow of the tree.

$$\frac{\text{length of tree shadow}}{\text{length of stick shadow}} \times \frac{\text{stick}}{\text{height}} = \frac{\text{tree}}{\text{height}}$$

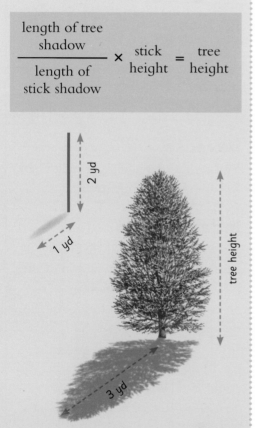

$$\frac{3 \text{ yd}}{1 \text{ yd}} \times 2 \text{ yd} = 6 \text{ yd (tree height)}$$

See **ratio, similar**

inequality

Where one quantity is less than or greater than another. In a math sentence, the following signs are used:

$<$ less than $\neq$ not equal to

$\leq$ less than or equal to

$>$ greater than

$\geq$ greater than or equal to

$$3 + 5 > 7$$

This inequation shows that three plus five is greater than seven.
See **equality, equation, greater than, less than, not equal**

infer

Come to a conclusion, or make a guess, based on observation or logic.
See **prediction**

infinite

Without bounds of size or number; unlimited, endless.

infinity

Symbol ∞
Endlessness.

input

See **number machine**

insignificant zeros

Unnecessary zeros in numbers.

05.2   wrong   **5.2**   correct

integers

Positive or negative whole numbers including zero.

> –5 –4 –3 –2 –1 0
> negative integers
>
> 0 +1 +2 +3 +4 +5
> positive integers

See **negative numbers, positive numbers, whole numbers**

interest

An amount of money given or charged by a bank.
1. The bank pays you interest for having money in a bank account.
2. Banks charge interest when you borrow money from them.

interest rate The amount paid or charged is often expressed as a yearly (annual) percentage of the amount saved or borrowed.

Oliver has $100 in his account.

The interest rate is 5% annually.

At the end of the year, Oliver receives 5% of $100, which is $5.00.

See **annual, percent, principal**

interior

The inside of something.

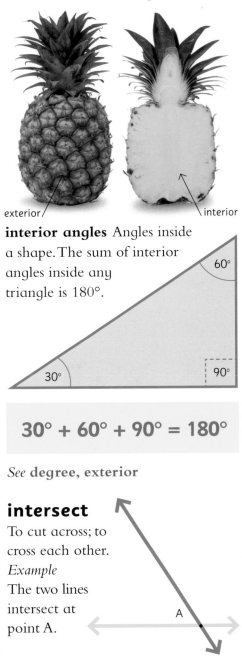

exterior / interior

interior angles Angles inside a shape. The sum of interior angles inside any triangle is 180°.

60°

30°

90°

> **30° + 60° + 90° = 180°**

See **degree, exterior**

intersect

To cut across; to cross each other.
Example
The two lines intersect at point A.

A

intersection

1. The place where two or more lines meet, such as an intersection of two streets.

intersection

2. The region where shapes overlap.

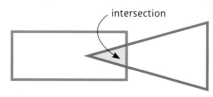

intersection

3. (Of sets) The set of elements that are common to both sets.

circles

blue shapes

intersection—blue circles

See **coordinates, origin, region, set, shape, Venn diagram**

interval

The amount of time, or distance, between two events or places.
Example There is a twenty-minute interval between the two movies.

inverse

The opposite or reverse of something.
inverse operation An operation that reverses the action of the original operation.
The inverse of addition is subtraction:
$$4 + 3 = 7 \qquad 7 - 3 = 4$$
The inverse of multiplication is division:
$$6 \times 3 = 18 \qquad 18 \div 3 = 6$$
See **addition, invert, operation**

invert

Turn upside down, reverse position.
Example
$\frac{1}{2}$ inverts to $\frac{2}{1}$ or 2.
$\frac{3}{4}$ inverts to $\frac{4}{3}$ or $1\frac{1}{3}$

irrational number

A number that cannot be written as a ratio between two whole numbers.
Example pi (π).
The value of $\pi \approx 3.141592643...$ but its exact value cannot be written down.
See **pi, ratio. rational number, real number**

isosceles triangle

A triangle that has two sides of the same length and two angles of the same size.

JjKk

joule

Symbol J

Unit of energy or work. It replaces the old unit, calorie.

See **calorie, kilojoule**

kilo

A prefix meaning a thousand.

kilogram

Symbol kg

The base unit of mass.

1 kg = 1,000 g

The mass of potatoes in the sack is 12 kg.

kilojoule   *Symbol* kJ

Used for measuring energy or work.

1 kilojoule = 1,000 joules

This piece of cake contains 2,000 kJ.

kiloliter   *Symbol* kl

A unit of volume (capacity) for measuring liquids.

1 kl = 1,000 l

Example

Five 200-liter oil drums hold one kiloliter.

kilometer   *Symbol* km

A unit of distance in metric. Long distances are measured in kilometers.

1 km = 1,000 m

See **distance, gram, mass, unit of measurement**

kite

A four-sided, 2-D shape (quadrilateral) where the two short sides are equal in length and the two long sides are equal in length. A kite has one line of symmetry.

See **quadrilateral, symmetry**

knot

Symbol kn

A measure of speed at sea and in flying, equal to traveling at a speed of one nautical mile per hour.

1 nautical mile = 1.15 miles (1.85 km)

See **speed**

Ll

leap year

A year with 366 days
instead of 365 days.
It occurs every four years.
In a leap year February
has 29 days instead of 28.
You can tell if a year is a leap year
by seeing if it can be divided
exactly by 4.

1979 ÷ 4 = 494 (r3)

1979 was not a leap year.

2020 ÷ 4 = 505

2020 is a leap year.

Century years are leap years only
if they are divisible by 400.
These are leap years:

1600, 2000, 2400

These are not leap years:

1500, 1700, 1800

See **remainder**

least

The smallest thing or amount
in a group.

$3.50

$5.20

$1.85

The toy car costs the least amount.

length

How long something is from end
to end.
1. The measure of distance.

The length of this ruler is 6 in (15 cm).
2. An interval of time.
Example
The length of recess is 40 minutes.
See **distance, interval**

less than

Symbol <
Not as much, smaller than.
An expression that shows which
number is smaller in a pair of numbers.

5 < 7

5 is less than 7.

See **greater than, inequality**

FEBRUARY

29

like terms

Similar, resembling each other. Like terms can be added and subtracted, but unlike terms cannot.

like terms

unlike terms

See **unlike terms, variable**

line

A thin mark with only one dimension. It can be straight or curved. A straight line is the shortest distance between two points.

line segment Part of a straight line.

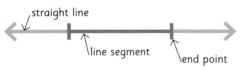

straight line

line segment

end point

linear A measurement in one dimension only.

See **curve, dimension, horizontal line, infinite, interval, vertical**

line graph

See **graph**

line of symmetry

Sometimes called the axis of symmetry, it is the line that divides something in half so that one half is the mirror image of the other half.

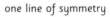

one line of symmetry

three lines of symmetry

A shape may have more than one line of symmetry.

See **asymmetry, axis, symmetry**

liter

Symbol l

A metric unit of capacity used to measure the volume of liquids or the capacity of containers. This carton of milk holds one liter.

See **capacity, unit of measurement, volume**

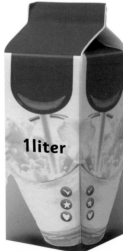

1 liter

a b c d e f g h i j k **l** m n o p q r s t u v w x y z

loss

If the selling price is lower than the cost price, the seller makes a loss.

A car dealer buys
a car for $10,000
and sells the
same car for $9,000

Since the selling price of the car is less than the buying price, the dealer takes a loss of $1,000

See **cost price, profit, selling price**

lowest common denominator (LCD)

The lowest number that can be divided exactly by the denominators of two or more fractions. Also known as the least common denominator.

Example

To find the LCD of

$$\frac{1}{4} \quad \text{and} \quad \frac{1}{10} \leftarrow \text{denominator}$$

you must find the lowest number that is divisible by both denominators (4 and 10). The lowest number into which 4 and 10 will divide exactly is 20. Therefore the lowest common denominator is 20.

Multiples of 4	Multiples of 10
4, 8, 12,	10, **20**,
16, **20**,	30, **40**,
24, 28, 32,	50...
36, **40** ...	

shows multiples of both 4 and 10

See **common denominator, denominator, fraction**

lowest common multiple (LCM)

The lowest number that can be divided by two or more numbers. Also known as the least common multiple.

Example

What is the LCM of 2 and 3?

Multiples of 2	Multiples of 3
2, 4, **6**,	3, **6**, 9
8, 10, **12**,	**12**, 15,
14, 16, **18** ...	**18**, 21...

shows common multiples of both 2 and 3

Common multiples of 2 and 3 are 6, 12, 18... The lowest common multiple of 2 and 3 is 6.

common multiple A number that can be divided by two or more other numbers without a remainder.

See **multiplication**

Mm

magic square

A puzzle in which the numbers are arranged in a square so that each row, column, and diagonal adds up to the same total.

Example

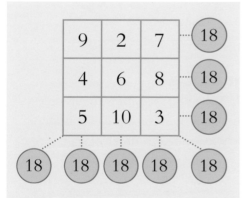

The number all columns, rows, and diagonals add up to is known as the magic constant. In this magic square, the magic constant is 18.

map

A drawing of a place. A map is often drawn to scale, which means that the area is drawn smaller but still keeps the same proportions.
See **scale drawing**

mapping

A joining or matching operation between two sets. Each member of the first set is assigned to only one member of the second set.

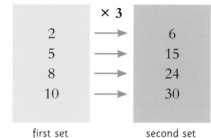

first set   second set

In the above example, 2 maps onto 6. 6 is called the image of 2.
See **arrow diagram,
one-to-one correspondence, set**

mass

The amount of matter contained in an object. Mass is measured in grams (g), kilograms (kg), and tons (t).
This girl has a mass of 28 kg. The word "weight" is commonly but incorrectly used instead of mass.
See **beam balance,
unit of measurement,
weight**

matching

See **arrow diagram,
one-to-one correspondence**

mathematical shorthand

Instead of using long sentences, mathematics uses numbers, symbols, formulas, and diagrams.

Example

The shorthand

$$a^2 + b^2 = c^2$$

says the same as:
"On a right–angled triangle, the square of the hypotenuse is equal to the sum of the squares of the other two sides."

See **formula**

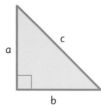

maximum

The greatest or biggest value.

Example The maximum temperature today was 84°F (29°C).

See **minimum**

maze

A puzzle with a complicated network of lines or paths.

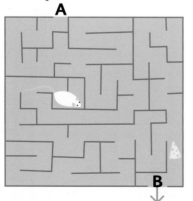

Follow the path from A to B without crossing any walls.

mean

The average of a set of scores. It is found by adding up all the scores and dividing the answer by the number of scores.

See **average**

measure

To find the size or amount of something.

Example
The book measures 15 in long.

15 in

See **unit of measurement**

median

In statistics, median is the middle measurement or score, when items are arranged in order of size.

Scores:

2, 2, 4, 5, 6, 8, 10

median = 5

Where there is no middle score, an average of the two central scores is taken.

Scores:

2, 3, 4, 8, 9, 10

median = (4 + 8) ÷ 2 = 6

See **average, mean, mode, score**

mega

Symbol M

Prefix (a word added to the start of a word) meaning one million.

megaliter *Symbol* Ml

A unit of capacity.

    1 megaliter = 1,000,000 liters

    1 Ml = 1,000,000 l

This swimming pool contains four megaliters (4 Ml) of water.

meter

Symbol m

The base unit of length in metric.

    1 m = 100 cm

    1 m = 1,000 mm

The giraffe is 5 meters in height.

The girl is 1 meter in height.

See **distance, unit of measurement**

metric system

A decimal system of weights and measures. The base unit for length is meter, for mass is kilogram, and for time is second.

See **standard unit of measuring, unit of measurement**

midpoint

A point in the middle of an interval.

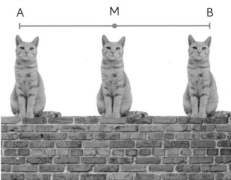

The point M is the midpoint of the interval (or distance) AB.

See **bisect, interval**

mile

An Imperial measure of length.

    1 mile ≈ 1.6 km

mileage

The distance in miles a vehicle travels using a certain amount of gas. Mileage is measured in miles per gallon (mpg). Mileage is also called fuel economy and can be measured in liters of gas per 100 kilometers.

See **gallon, mile**

milli

Symbol m
Prefix meaning one-thousandth.

$$\frac{1}{1,000}$$

milligram *Symbol* mg
A unit of mass equal to $\frac{1}{1,000}$ of a gram.

| $1 \text{ mg} = \frac{1}{1,000} \text{ gram}$ | $1 \text{ mg} = 0.001 \text{ gram}$ |

See **gram, mass**

milliliter *Symbol* ml
A metric unit of capacity that is equal to one-thousandth of a liter.

| 1,000 ml = 1 liter |

A teaspoon holds 5 ml.   This bottle holds 1 liter.   This bucket holds 9 liters.

Note: One milliliter of water at 4°C has a mass of one gram.
See **liter, volume**

millimeter *Symbol* mm
A metric unit of length.

| 1,000 mm = 1 meter |

See **meter, length**

0
10 mm
20 mm

million

One thousand thousands:

1,000,000

millionth One part out of a million.

$$\frac{1}{1,000,000}$$

minimum

The smallest or least value.
Example The minimum temperature in July was 39°F (4°C).
See **maximum**

minuend

A number from which another number is to be subtracted.

$$29 - 7 = 22$$

minuend   subtrahend   difference

In this example, 29 is the minuend.
See **difference, subtraction**

minus

Symbol −
1. Subtract or take away.
Example Eight minus two is written as $8 - 2$ and means two subtracted from eight.

$$8 - 2 = 6$$

2. A symbol to mark negative numbers.

$$-1, -2, -3, -4...$$

Negative 1, negative 2, negative 3, negative 4...
See **integers, negative numbers, subtraction**

minute

See **time**

mirror image

A reflection, as in a mirror.

See **image, reflection**

mixed number

A whole number and a fraction.

$$1\frac{1}{2} \qquad 3\frac{5}{6}$$

This is another way of writing an improper fraction.

$$\frac{3}{2} = 1\frac{1}{2} \qquad \frac{35}{30} = 1\frac{5}{30} = 1\frac{1}{6}$$

See **fraction, improper fraction, whole numbers**

möbius strip

Also spelt as moebius.
A surface with only one side, made by half-twisting a strip of paper and joining the ends together. If you draw a line along the middle of the strip, when you come back to the start, you will have drawn on both sides of the paper. If you cut along the line, you get one big strip.

mode

In statistics, the score that occurs most often in a collection.
For the scores:

1, 1, 2, 4, 4, 6, 6, 6, 6, 7, 7, 7, 8, 10

6 is the mode.
See **average, mean, median**

model

A smaller 3-D copy of an actual or designed object.

This is a model of an airplane.

See **three-dimensional**

month

A period of time. A month has 28, 29, 30, or 31 days.

more

Greater in amount.
Example $4 is more than $3.

most

The greatest amount.
Example Anna has 20 cents, Ben has 35 cents, and Joe has 5 cents. Ben has the most.

multi

A prefix (part of the beginning of a word) meaning "more than one," such as in the word multiplication.

multiplication

multiply, multiplying
Symbol ×

A quick way of adding up lots of the same number (repeated addition) or adding equal groups of things together. You can multiply whole numbers, fractions, and decimals.
The symbol "×" means groups of, multiplied by.

This shows:
2 groups of 3 eggs: $2 \times 3 = 6$
or 3 multiplied by 2: $3 \times 2 = 6$
or 3 made 2 times bigger = 6

multiple A number that can be divided exactly by another number.
Multiples of two are:

$$2, 4, 6, 8, 10, 12...$$

Multiples of three are:

$$3, 6, 9, 12, 15, 18...$$

multiplicand The number that is being multiplied.

multiplicative identity When a number is multiplied by 1, the answer (product) is equal to the original number.

$$7 \times 1 = 7$$
$$1 \times 138 = 138$$

It can be used when converting a fraction to an equivalent form.

$$\frac{2}{3} = \frac{?}{12} \qquad \text{The same as} \times 1$$

$$\frac{2}{3} \times \frac{4}{4} = \frac{8}{12}$$

To convert $\frac{2}{3}$ to $\frac{8}{12}$ $\frac{2}{3}$ is multiplied by 1, or $\frac{4}{4}$.
We use 4 because $3 \times 4 = 12$.
The numerators (top numbers) are then multiplied, to give the answer $\frac{8}{12}$.

multiplier The number by which another number is multiplied.

$$8 \times 7 = 56$$

multiplicand   multiplier   product

multiply Perform the process of multiplication or repeated addition.

$$5 \times 7 = 35$$

See **addition, division, fractions, lowest common multiple, operation, product**
See **multiplication table on p.128**

Nn

natural number

One of the counting numbers.

1, 2, 3, 4, 5, 6, 7, 8, 9...

See **counting number, positive numbers**

nautical mile

Unit of length as used on planes, boats, and ships. A nautical mile is based on the circumference of the Earth. One nautical mile equals 6,076 feet (1,852 meters) or 1.15 miles (1.852 km).
See **knot**

negative numbers

Numbers less than zero. Negative numbers are written with the minus sign (–) in front of them.

-1, -2, -3, -4, -5, etc
-0.1, -0.2, etc

negative numbers
on a number line

See **integers, minus, number line, positive numbers, zero**

net

A flat pattern that can be cut out, folded, and glued together to make a 3-D model of a solid.

Net of a cube

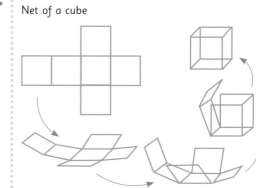

Net of a square-based pyramid

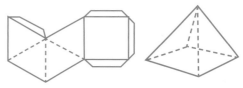

nonagon

A 2-D shape (polygon) with nine sides and nine angles.

regular nonagon   irregular nonagons

See **polygon**

none

Nothing. Not one. Not any.

I have 2 apples.   I have none.
See **zero**

not equal

Symbol ≠

$$4 \neq 5$$

Four is not equal to five.
See **inequality**

nothing

Symbol 0
Not one. Having not a thing.
Not anything.
See **none, zero**

number expander

A folded strip of paper used to learn place value.

number line

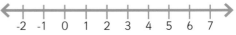

A line on which equally spaced points are marked and numbered. It shows the position of a number. Operations with numbers can be shown on a number line.

Add three and four:

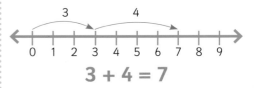

$$3 + 4 = 7$$

Subtract five from nine:

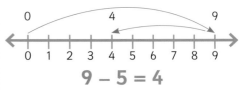

$$9 - 5 = 4$$

See **operation, order**

number

How many things. A measure of quantity. Numbers are grouped into many different sets:

1. Natural (counting) numbers:

$$1, 2, 3, 4, 5, 6 \ldots$$

2. Whole numbers:

$$0, 1, 2, 3, 4, 5 \ldots$$

3. Integers:

$$\ldots -4, -3, -2, -1,$$
$$0, +1, +2, +3 \ldots$$

number machine

Number machines can carry out operations such as addition, subtraction, multiplication, and division. Calculators and computers are types of number machines.

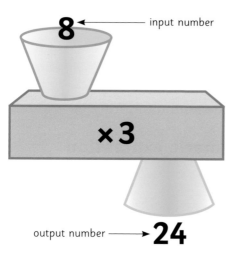

8 ← input number

×3

output number → **24**

1. The number 8 is put into the machine. This is the input number.
2. The number is multiplied by 3. This is the rule.
3. What comes out of the number machine is the answer.

See **rule**

number pattern

See **pattern**

number sentence

A statement about numbers, usually in symbols rather than words. A number sentence can be true or false, open or closed.

$$6 + 7 = 13 \quad \text{(true)}$$

$$4 \neq 9 \quad \text{(true)}$$

$$5 + ? = 9 \quad \text{(open)}$$

$$7 + 9 = 10 \quad \text{(false)}$$

$$3 + 1 < 3 \times 1 \quad \text{(false)}$$

$$7 - ? = 0 \quad \text{(open)}$$

See **inequality, open number sentence**

4. Rational numbers that include fractions and ratios:

$\frac{25}{100}$ **1:4**

four quarters of a cake

5. Other kinds of numbers include complex, composite, prime, odd, even, square, triangular, rectangular numbers, etc.
See **composite number, even number, irrational number, odd number, prime number**

a b c d e f g h i j k l m **n** o p q r s t u v w x y z

number track

A track, as used in board games, where the sections are numbered.

numerator

The top number in a fraction. It tells how many parts of the whole there are.

$$\frac{3}{4}$$

3 ← numerator
4 ← denominator

$\frac{3}{4}$ means there are 3 parts out of a possible four parts.
See **denominator, fraction**

numeric expression

A number expression without an equals sign. It is also called an arithmetic expression.

$$4 + 6$$

numeral

A symbol used to represent a number.

5 is the numeral that represents the number five.

5 apples

V The Roman numeral for the number five is V.

numeration A system of symbols used to represent numbers.
Our system uses the symbols:

See **Hindu–Arabic, Roman numerals, symbol**

0, 1, 2, 3, 4, 5, 6, 7, 8, and 9.

oblong

A quadrilateral (a two-dimensional, four-sided shape) with two pairs of equal and parallel sides and four right angles. Another word for a rectangle.

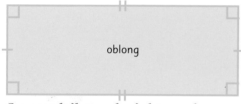

oblong

See **quadrilateral, right angle**

obtuse angle

An angle bigger than 90°, but smaller than 180°.

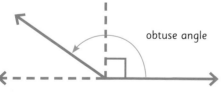

obtuse angle

obtuse triangle A triangle with one obtuse angle.

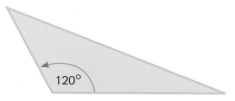

120°

See **acute, angle, triangle**

o'clock

A short way of saying "of the clock" when telling the time.

octagon

A 2-D shape (polygon) with 8 straight sides and 8 angles.

regular octagon

irregular octagons

See **plane shape, polygon**

octahedron

A 3-D shape (polyhedron) with 8 faces. A regular octahedron is made of 8 equilateral triangles.

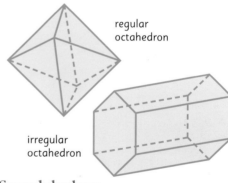

regular octahedron

irregular octahedron

See **polyhedron**

odd number

A number that cannot be divided exactly by 2. Odd numbers finish with 1, 3, 5, 7, or 9.

See **even number**

one-dimensional

A figure that only has length.

1-D figures

A line has only one dimension.
See **dimension, plane**

one-to-one ratio

Matching between two sets where each member of one set is paired with one member of the other set.

Cup and saucer

Set A = Grandpa   Jamil   Dad

↕   ↕   ↕

Set B =   tongs   bun   sausage

See **arrow diagram, mapping, set**

open curve

See **curve**

open number sentence

A mathematical sentence that contains numbers and variables (unknowns). It can be an equation (both parts are equal) or an inequality (parts are not equal).

> Equation
> $$5 + \Delta = 10$$

> Inequality
> $$7 + a > 5$$

See **equation, inequality, number sentence, variable**

operation

There are four arithmetic operations: addition, subtraction, multiplication, and division.
See **addition, arithmetic, basic facts, division, multiplication, subtraction**

operators

The signs used in operations. These are:

$$+ \quad - \quad \times \quad \div$$

opposite numbers

Two numbers that add up to zero.

$$-5 + 5 = 0$$

The opposite of −5 is 5.

order

To arrange in a pattern or a sequence according to size, value, etc. A pattern or sequence.

Rabbits ordered from smallest to largest.

See **ascending order, descending order, pattern, sequence**

ordered pair

An x-coordinate and a y-coordinate written as a pair, with the x-coordinate first.

Note: (3, 5) is not the same as (5, 3).

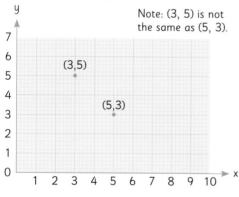

See **coordinates**

order of operations

Used when sorting complicated number sentences.

1. Number sentences with grouping symbols. Calculations inside the parentheses or brackets are done first.

Example

$$5 + \{10 - (4 \times 2)\}$$
$$= 5 + \{10 - (8)\}$$
$$= 5 + \{2\} = 7$$

2. When there are no grouping symbols, start from the left, insert parentheses around multiplication and division, then calculate them. Then start again from the left and do additions and subtractions.

Example

$$48 \div 3 + 2 - 4 \times 3$$
$$= (48 \div 3) + 2 - (4 \times 3)$$
$$= 16 + 2 - 12$$
$$= 18 - 12 = 6$$

Note: To help remember the order of operations, think PEDMAS: Parentheses, Exponents, Division, Multiplication, Addition, Subtraction. *See* **brackets, operation**

ordinal number

A number that indicates position.

1st   2nd   3rd   4th   5th

See **cardinal number**

a b c d e f g h i j k l m n **o** p q r s t u v w x y z

origin

A point at which something begins.

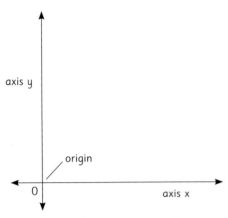

The point where axes x and y intersect is called the origin and is marked 0. Its coordinates are (0, 0).
See **axis, coordinates, intersect, ordered pair**

ounce

Symbol oz
An Imperial unit of weight or mass.
16 oz = 1 pound (lb)

outcome

The result of an experiment where the end result is not known in advance.
Example
There are two possible outcomes of tossing a coin: either heads or tails.
See **event, probability**

outlier

Part of a set of data that stands out from the rest.
Example
In the set of scores 94%, 87%, 92%, and 53%, the outlier is 53%, as it is outside the range of the other data.

output

See **number machine**

oval

1. An egg-shaped figure that is symmetrical around one axis. One end is more pointed than the other.

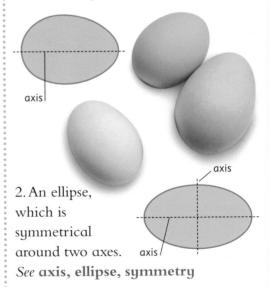

2. An ellipse, which is symmetrical around two axes.
See **axis, ellipse, symmetry**

overdraft

The result of removing more money out of a bank account than you actually have in it.
See **credit, debit**

Pp

pace

The distance between your feet when you take a step, measured from heel to heel. It is an arbitrary unit for estimating distances.

Example

Jack's pace measures 22 in (56 cm).

1 pace

See **arbitrary unit, distance, estimate**

pair

Two things that belong together.

a pair of socks

palindrome

A number, word, or sentence that reads the same forward as backward.

1991   19.9.1991   madam

parallel lines

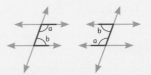

Symbols

Two or more lines that go in exactly the same direction. Parallel lines always remain the same distance apart; they never meet.

Train tracks are parallel.

If parallel lines are crossed by a straight line, pairs of angles are formed:

1. Corresponding angles (they make an F-shape) are equal.

2. Alternate angles (they make a Z-shape) are equal.

3. Cointerior angles (they make a U-shape) add up to 180°.

See **vertically opposite angles**

parallelogram

A four-sided figure (quadrilateral) in which both pairs of opposite sides are parallel and equal, and the opposite angles are equal.

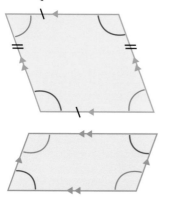

The arrow marks  show which pairs of lines are parallel. The marks \ \\ show which lines are of the same length.

A right-angled parallelogram is a rectangle.

See **parallel lines, quadrilateral, rectangle**

parentheses

Curved brackets. ( )

partition

Another name for sharing.
See **division**

Pascal's triangle

An arrangement of numbers used in probability. After the second line, each number in the triangle is made by adding together the two numbers directly above it.

pattern

A repeated design or arrangement using shapes, colors, numbers, etc.

1. Shape pattern

2. A number pattern is a sequence of numbers formed by following a rule:

1, 4, 7, 10...   (rule: add three)

See **rule, sequence**

penny

Plural pennies

A coin equal to one-hundredth of a dollar. The plural is "pennies," but when referring to a sum of money, you say "cents."

pentagon

A 2-D shape (polygon) with five straight sides and five angles.

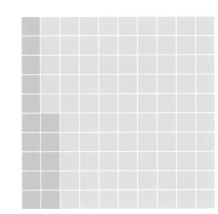

regular pentagon

See **polygon**   irregular pentagon

percent (percentage)

Symbol %

A number out of one hundred.

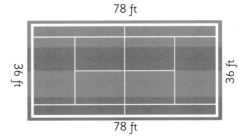

40% of the pins have been knocked over.

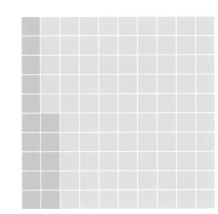

This is a "hundred square." Fifteen out of the hundred little squares have been colored in. They represent:

$$\frac{15}{100} = 0.15 = 15\%$$

fraction decimal fraction percentage

See **decimal fraction, fraction**

perimeter

The distance around a closed shape, or the length of its boundary.
To find the perimeter of a shape, add the lengths of all its sides.

78 ft

36 ft   36 ft

78 ft

The perimeter of a tennis court is:
78 ft + 36 ft + 78 ft + 36 ft = 228 ft

See **boundary**

permutation

An ordered arrangement or sequence of a group of objects.

Example

Three shapes can be arranged in six different ways, so they have six permutations:

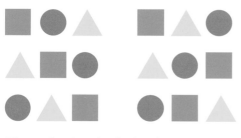

The order in which the shapes are arranged is important in a permutation. When the order is not important, the arrangement is called a combination.

See **combination**

perpendicular

Forming a right angle.

perpendicular height A line drawn from the top (vertex) of a figure to the base opposite at a 90° angle.

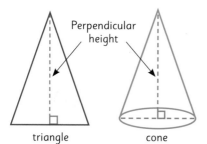

triangle   cone

perpendicular lines Lines that meet or intersect to make right angles.

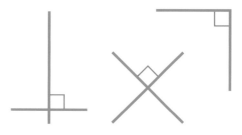

See **apex, cone, line, triangle, vertex**

perspective

When drawing, we can show depth by running all parallel lines to one or several points on the horizon. These points are called vanishing points. This makes a two-dimensional drawing looks three-dimensional. We say it has perspective.

vanishing point

See **converging lines, horizon, three-dimensional, two-dimensional**

pi

Symbol π

The number you get when you divide a circle's circumfrence by its diameter.

$$\pi = \frac{\text{circumference}}{\text{diameter}}$$

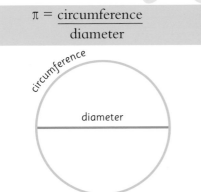

The approximate value of π is 3.14. It is an infinite (endless) decimal. The exact value cannot be worked out.

See **circle, diameter, infinite, radius, ratio**

pictograph

pictogram, picture graph

See **graph**

pie graph

See **graph**

pint

Symbol pt

An Imperial unit used to measure the capacity of liquids.

8 pints = 1 gallon

1 pint = approximately 0.5 liters

place holder

1. A symbol that holds the place for an unknown number.

In $w + 3 = 7$, w is the place holder.
In $\star - 6 = 10$, $\star$ is the place holder.

2. Zero, when used with other digits, is used as a place holder. In the United States, this is called the identity element in addition.

6,800

The zeros shows us that the 6 means six thousands, the 8 means eight hundreds, and that there are no ones and no tens.

See **digit, equation, variable**

place value

The value of each part of a number depends on its place or position in that number.

hundreds	tens	ones
4	8	6

In the number 486, 6 means six ones, 8 means eight tens, and 4 means four hundreds.

See **decimal place value system, digit, value**

plan

1. To prepare ahead of time.
Example Plan for a vacation.
2. A diagram of an object as seen from above.

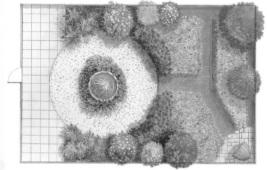

garden plan

See **cross-section of a solid, diagram, front view, side view**

plane

A flat surface, such as the floor of a house or a wall. A plane extends infinitely in all directions.

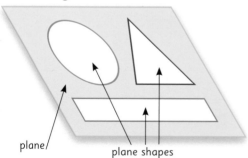

plane
plane shapes

plane shape A closed shape that can be drawn on a flat surface. All two-dimensional objects are plane shapes (planar figures), because they can be drawn in one plane.

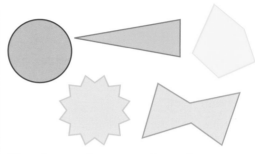

The shapes above are plane shapes.
See **dimension, infinite, two-dimensional**

plus

Symbol +
The name of the symbol that represents addition.

$$4 + 6 = 10$$

See **addition**

p.m. (post meridiem)

See **time**

point

1. A small dot on a surface, which has no dimension.

.P

The dot shows where the point P is.

2. In money, a point separates the units of currency (such as dollars) from the parts of the units (cents).

$4.50

The point shows 4 = four dollars and 50 = fifty cents.

See **cent, decimal point, dollar**

polygon

A 2-D (plane) shape that has three or more straight sides.

regular polygon A polygon with equal sides and angles.

irregular polygon A polygon where the sides and angles are not all equal.

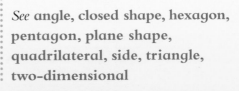

See **angle, closed shape, hexagon, pentagon, plane shape, quadrilateral, side, triangle, two-dimensional**

polyhedron

Plural polyhedrons or polyhedra

A 3-D shape with flat (plane) faces.

regular polyhedron

All faces are regular polygons and all are the same size.

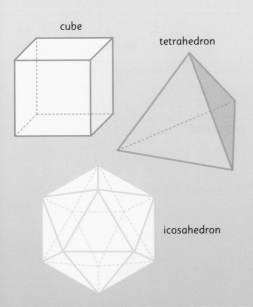

cube

tetrahedron

icosahedron

irregular polyhedron

Faces are different sizes and angles and are not all equal.

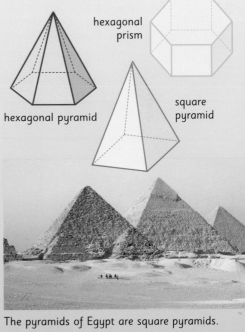

hexagonal prism

hexagonal pyramid

square pyramid

The pyramids of Egypt are square pyramids.

See **cube, icosahedron, prism, pyramid, tetrahedron**

a b c d e f g h i j k l m n o **p** q r s t u v w x y z

polyomino

A plane shape made of squares of the same size, with each square connected to at least one of the others by a common edge.

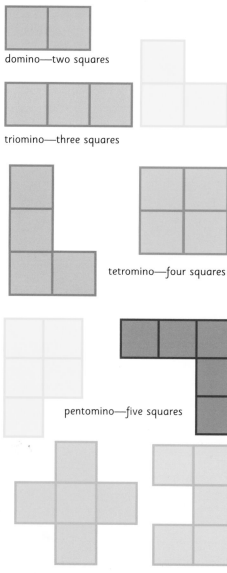

domino—two squares

triomino—three squares

tetromino—four squares

pentomino—five squares

See **plane, two-dimensional**

position

The place where something is. On, under, above, behind, in front of, between, next to, and outside all describe the position of something.

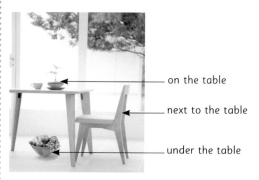

on the table

next to the table

under the table

See **coordinates**

positive numbers

Numbers greater than zero. We sometimes write the plus sign (+) in front of them.

−4 −3 −2 −1 0 **+1 +2 +3 +4**

See **integers, negative numbers, plus, zero**

pound

1. *Symbol* lb
An Imperial unit of weight equal to 16 ounces. There are 2,000 pounds in a ton.
2. *Symbol* £
A unit of money used in the UK divided into 100 pennies.
See **ounce**

power (of a number)

The power of a number (also called the index or exponent) shows how many times a number is multiplied by itself.
The power of 2^4 is 4.
It means $2 \times 2 \times 2 \times 2 = 16$.
You say "two to the power of four."
When the power is zero, the value is one. $10^0 = 1$ $1,000^0 = 1$
See **cubed number, index, square of a number**

prediction

An estimate. In mathematics we may predict, or estimate, possible answers.

prefix

A word added to the start of a unit that tells us how large a measure is.
Kilogram means one thousand grams.

prime factor

A prime number that divides exactly into a given number.
2, 3, and 5 are the prime factors of 30. (10 is also a factor of 30, but not a prime factor.)

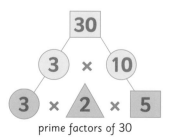

prime factors of 30

prime factorization

Finding the prime numbers you need to multiply together to get the original number.
1. 12 is divisible by 2, 3, 4, and 6.
2. Only 2 and 3 are prime numbers.
3. This means the prime factorization of 12 is:
$2 \times 2 \times 3 = 12$
See **division, factor tree, factors, inverse, multiplication, prime number**

prime number

A counting number that can only be divided by one and itself.

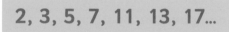

2, 3, 5, 7, 11, 13, 17...

The factors (numbers that divide another number without leaving a remainder) of two are 2 and 1.
The factors of five are 5 and 1.
Note 1 is not a prime number.
The largest prime number found so far has 12,978,189 digits!
See **composite number, counting number, factors**

principal

The amount borrowed or invested is called the principal.
Example Joe borrowed $100 from a bank. The principal is $100.

prism

A 3-D shape with two parallel faces that are polygons, and the same in shape and size.

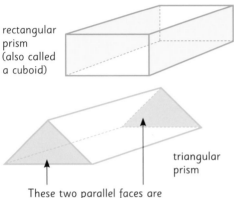

rectangular prism (also called a cuboid)

triangular prism

These two parallel faces are the same shape and size.

All cuboids are prisms.
See **cuboid, face, parallel lines, polygon, polyhedron, three-dimensional**

probability

The likelihood, or chance, of an event happening. There are different types of chance: likely, unlikely, equally likely, impossible, or certain.

1, 2, 3, 4, 5, and 6 are equally likely when you throw a die.

See **certain, chance, event**

problem solving

Using mathematical ideas to find solutions in new situations.

trial and error Selecting a possible answer to a problem, then trying it out to see if it works. If it does not work, another way must be tried.

work backward When you start with the end result and go backward, doing the opposite operation for each step.

See **operation**

product

The answer to a multiplication problem.

$$3 \times 2 = 6$$

multiplicand   multiplier   product

See **multiplication**

profit

When the selling price is higher than the price the seller paid originally for something, the difference is the profit.

A car dealer buys a car for $10,000. He sells the same car for $12,000. The selling price is $2,000 higher than the buying price, so the dealer's profit is $2,000.

See **cost price, loss, selling price**

progression

A sequence of numbers following a given rule. The numbers increase or decrease in a constant way.

1. If the rule is "add a number" or "subtract a number" it is called an arithmetic progression.

> Rule: add 3
>
> **1, 4, 7, 10, 13, 16...**

2. If the rule is "multiply by a number" or "divide by a number" it is called a geometric progression.

> Rule: multiply by 4
>
> **1, 4, 16, 64...**

See **decrease, increase, pattern, sequence**

projection

The transformation of one shape or picture to another.

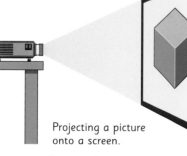

Projecting a picture onto a screen.

See **transformation**

proper fraction

A proper fraction is where the numerator (top number) is less than the denominator (bottom number).

Example

$\frac{4}{5}$ and $\frac{36}{100}$ are proper fractions.

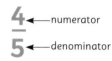

4 ◄— numerator
5 ◄— denominator

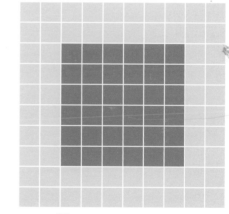

$\frac{36}{100}$ is a proper fraction.

See **denominator, fraction, improper fraction, numerator**

property

A characteristic of an object, such as its length or weight.

See **attribute, classification, proportion**

a b c d e f g h i j k l m n o p q r s t u v w x y z

proportion

Part of a whole, written as a fraction, percentage, or decimal.
Example The drink is $\frac{1}{4}$ (25%, 0.25) syrup and $\frac{3}{4}$ (75%, 0.75) water.

direct proportion When two quantities increase or decrease by the same amount, or ratio, the two ratios are equal.

Three cans of paint are enough to paint one wall, so six cans of paint are needed for two walls.

indirect proportion Two quantities are in indirect proportion when as one gets bigger, the other gets smaller by the same ratio.

It takes one person four hours to mow the lawn. This means it will take two people two hours, and four people one hour.

number of people	1	2	4	8	16
time in hours	4	2	1	$\frac{1}{2}$	$\frac{1}{4}$

in proportion Maps are in proportion to the actual ground. The amount the map is scaled down by is written as a ratio, such as 1:50,000. This means that 1 cm on the map is 50,000 cm of the actual ground.
50,000 cm = 500 m = 0.5 km
See **inverse, ratio**

protractor

An instrument used to measure and draw angles.

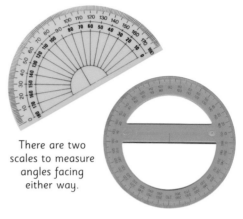

There are two scales to measure angles facing either way.

prove

Test the correctness of a calculation.

pyramid

A 3-D shape that has any type of polygon for a base, and triangular sides.

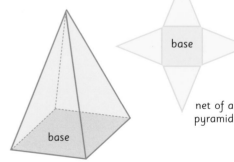

base

net of a pyramid

base

This pyramid has a square base. The other faces are matching (congruent) triangles.
See **base, congruent, face, net, polygon, polyhedron**

Qq

quadrant

1. A quarter of a circle.

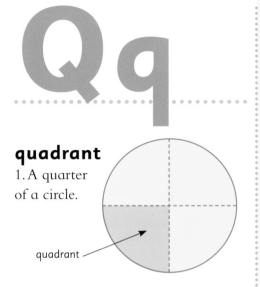

quadrant

2. In coordinate geometry, the space between the x-axis and y-axis is called a quadrant. If we extend the x-axis and the y-axis we can see all 4 quadrants of the number plane. Quadrants are numbered in a counterclockwise direction.

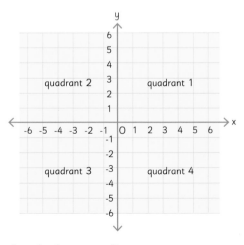

See **circle, coordinates, geometry, ordered pair**

quadrilateral

A 2-D shape (polygon) with four sides and four angles.

Some quadrilaterals are:

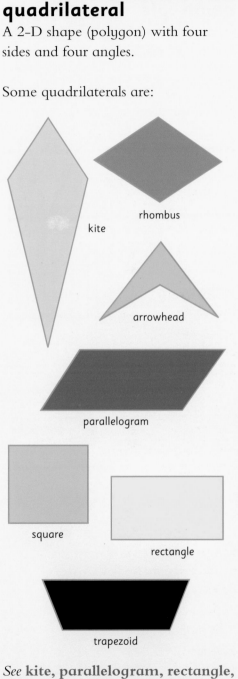

kite

rhombus

arrowhead

parallelogram

square

rectangle

trapezoid

See **kite, parallelogram, rectangle, rhombus, square, trapezoid**

quadruple

Increase the amount four times.
Quadruple $20 means:

$$4 \times \$20 = \$80$$

See **double, treble**

quantity

The amount
or number
of something.

The total
quantity of oil
in the bottles
is 3 liters.

quart

Symbol qt

An Imperial unit used to measure
the capacity of liquids.

4 quarts = 1 gallon

quotient

The answer to a division problem.

$$10 \div 2 = 5$$

↑   ↑   ↑

dividend   divisor   quotient

Five is the quotient.

quotition

Another name for grouping.

See **division, grouping**

quarter

One of four equal parts.

$\frac{1}{4}$ of the square is
shaded dark orange.

Each quarter of the pizza
has a different topping.

The orange
has been
cut into
quarters.

One quarter can
be written in
different ways:

0.25 decimal

$\frac{1}{4}$ fraction

25% percentage

radius

Plural radii

A straight line that measures the distance from the center of a circle or sphere to its edge.

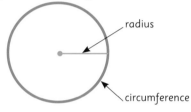

See **center, circle, diameter, line, sphere**

random sample

A statistics term. A part or portion that is chosen by chance to represent the whole.

range

The difference between the largest and the smallest number in a set.

The smallest number is 2.
The largest number is 8.
8 - 2 = 6.
The range is 6.

rate

When one amount (quantity) is compared to another.

Example

Sixty miles per hour (60 mph) compares miles to hours. It indicates the speed of travel.

See **comparison**

ratio

Symbol **:**

A way of comparing amounts (quantities). One quantity is expressed as a part of another.

Example

To make a pitcher of orange juice, mix 1 part of juice concentrate to 3 parts of water. This is a ratio of 1 : 3 (1 is juice concentrate and 3 is water).

3 parts water

1 part juice

The order of the numbers is important—here, the ratio of juice concentrate to water is 1 : 3, not 3 : 1.

See **comparison**

rational number

A number that can be written as a fraction, where the top and bottom of the fraction are whole numbers.

$$0.5 = \frac{1}{2}$$
$$8 = \frac{8}{1}$$

1. It can be represented by decimal numbers that end (terminate).

$$\frac{3}{4} = 0.75$$

2. It can also be represented by numbers that repeat.

$$\frac{2}{3} = 0.6666\ldots \text{ or } 0.\bar{6}$$

See **decimal, fraction, repeating decimal**

ray

A line that has a starting point but no end. It extends in one direction only.

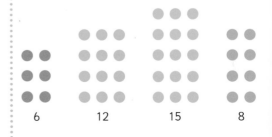

Sun

a ray of sunlight

See **line**

real number

The set of real numbers is made up of all rational and irrational numbers. All real numbers are found on the number line.
See **irrational number, number line, rational number**

reciprocal

A fraction made by swapping over the denominator and numerator.
Examples
1. Since we can write 4 as $\frac{4}{1}$, the reciprocal of 4 is $\frac{1}{4}$.
2. The reciprocal of $\frac{2}{3}$ is $\frac{3}{2}$ or $1\frac{1}{2}$.

rectangle

A quadrilateral (2-D, four-sided shape) with two pairs of equal and parallel sides, and four right angles.

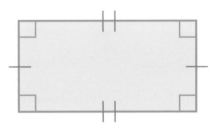

A rectangle is also called an oblong.
See **parallel lines, quadrilateral, right angle**

rectangular number

A number that can be represented by dots arranged in a rectangle.

6   12   15   8

rectangular prism

A 3-D shape (polyhedron) with a rectangular base. Most boxes are rectangular prisms.

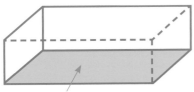

rectangle

See **polyhedron, prism, rectangle**

recurring decimal

See **repeating decimal**

reduce

To simplify or make smaller. To express a fraction in its simplest form.
Example
$\frac{2}{12}$ can be reduced to $\frac{1}{6}$.
See **canceling, fraction transformation**

reflection

The mirror image of an object.

mirror

See **flip, mirror image**

reflex angle

An angle greater than a straight angle (180°).

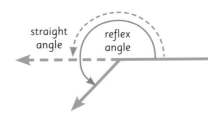

straight angle

reflex angle

See **angle, revolution, straight angle**

region

plane region All the points inside a closed shape together with all the points on the edge of the shape.
solid region All the points inside a closed area together with all the points on the surface.
Examples

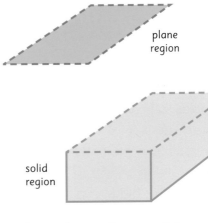

plane region

solid region

See **boundary, plane, solid, surface**

regroup

Exchange.

Example

Twelve unit blocks can be regrouped (exchanged) into 1 long block (a group of 10 units) and 2 units.

See **base 10 blocks, carrying, exchange, group**

regular shape

See **polygon**

relation

relationship

The connection between a pair of objects, measures, numbers, etc.

2 is half of 4.

The relation between pairs of numbers can be presented as an equation. The relation between the two rows in this table is $y = x + 5$.

x	1	2	3	4	5
y	6	7	8	9	10

remainder

The amount left over when a number does not divide exactly into another number.

$7 \div 2 =$ can be written as $2\overline{)7}$

2 can go into 6 exactly three times, but not 7, so we write 3 above the 7.

Then we take 6 away from 7 to find out the remainder.

There are different ways of writing the remainder in the answer.

1. *Question:* Five boys share 128 marbles. How many marbles does each boy get? *Answer:* Each boy gets 25 marbles. Three marbles are left over.

2. *Question*: Share $128 between five girls. *Answer:* Each girl gets $25 and $\frac{3}{5}$ of a dollar, that is $25 and 60 cents.

repeating decimal

A decimal with a digit or sequence of digits that repeats indefinitely.

0.666... or 0.6̄

This dash indicates that the digit repeats.

reverse

The opposite way around.

The reverse of A B C is C B A

reverse operation

The opposite of an operation.

Example

Addition is the reverse of subtraction.

See **inverse**

revolution

One complete turn. There are 360°
and four right angles in one revolution.

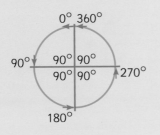

See **angle, right angle**

rhombus

A parallelogram with four equal
sides and two pairs of equal angles.

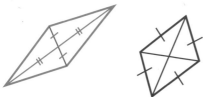

See **diamond, parallelogram**

Roman numerals

The Roman system of numbering
where numbers are represented
by letters.
I = 1, V = 5, X = 10, L = 50, C = 100
D = 500, M = 1,000.

Examples

$$2,000 = MM$$
$$2,002 = MMII$$

rotation

rotate
A turning
movement
around a
fixed point.

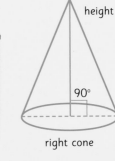

quarter
turn
(90°
rotation)

fixed
point

half turn
(180°
rotation)

three-quarter turn
(270° rotation)

right angle

Symbol ⌐→
An angle measuring exactly 90°.

right 3-D shape A solid with an
end or base that is 90° to its height,
such as a right cone.

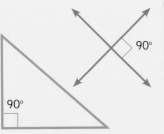

90°

90°

height

height

right-angled triangle
A triangle with a right angle.

right cone

90°

See **angle, cone**

a b c d e f g h i j k l m n o p q r s t u v w x y z

rotational symmetry

A shape has rotational symmetry if it can fit into its outline at least once when it is turned a complete turn (rotation) around a central point.

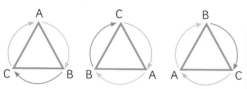

An equilateral triangle has rotational symmetry.

rounding

Writing a number as an approximation by replacing it with the nearest significant figure (usually one that can be divided by 10) to make it easier to work with.

Example

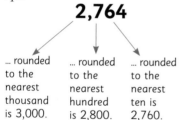

2,764

... rounded to the nearest thousand is 3,000.

... rounded to the nearest hundred is 2,800.

... rounded to the nearest ten is 2,760.

Rounding down
Numbers ending in 1, 2, 3, and 4 round down to the lower significant number: 54 rounded down is 50.

Rounding up
Numbers ending in 5, 6, 7, 8, and 9 round up to the higher significant number: 55 rounded up is 60.

See **accurate, estimate, significant figure**

route

A path or direction leading from one place to another.

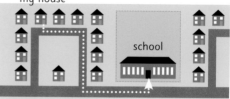

my route to school

row

Things arranged horizontally so that they make a line.
Example A row of numbers:

4, 5, 6, 7, 8, 9, ...

See **column, horizontal line**

rule

1. An instruction to do something in a particular way.

The rule for this sequence is "add 3."

2. To draw a line using a ruler.
ruler A device for drawing straight lines and measuring length.

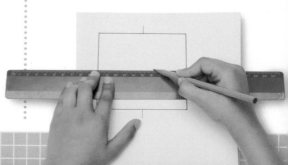

Ss

same

Identical, alike, unchanged, not different.
See **congruent**

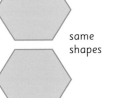

same shapes

sample

A selection taken from a larger group so that you can find out something about the larger group.
Example
A sample of children were asked about their favorite foods.

sample space

A term used in probability. It shows all the possible results (outcomes) of an experiment. There may be a small or large number of possible sample spaces.

Activity	Sample space
Rolling a die	{1, 2, 3, 4, 5, 6}
Tossing a coin	{Heads, tails}

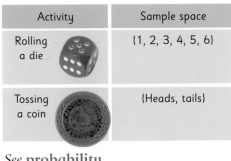

See **probability**

scale

1. Equally spaced markings on a measuring device. A thermometer, a ruler, and a balance each have a scale marked on them to measure temperature, length, and mass.

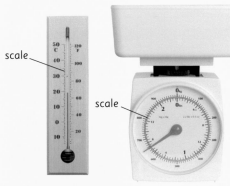

scale

scale

2. A number line used on a graph.

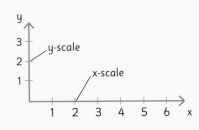

y-scale

x-scale

3. The scale on a map or a plan shows the ratio for making things larger or smaller.

Scale of kilometers
1 cm = 10 km

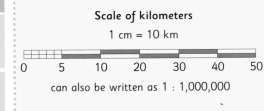

| 0 | 5 | 10 | 20 | 30 | 40 | 50 |

can also be written as 1 : 1,000,000

See **balance, graph, number line, ruler, thermometer**

a b c d e f g h i j k l m n o p q **r** **s** t u v w x y z

scale drawing

A drawing or plan on which the real object is made bigger or smaller while keeping the same proportions.

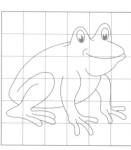

The drawing on the right has been scaled down on a scale of 1 to 2 or 1 : 2.

See **proportion, ratio**

scalene triangle

A triangle that has sides of different lengths and three different angles.

See **triangle**

scales

Instruments used for finding or comparing weights or masses.

bathroom scales

a balance for comparing masses

See **balance, mass, spring balance, weight**

scatter plot

A graph of plotted points that shows a relationship between two sets of information (data), one along the x-axis and one along the y-axis.

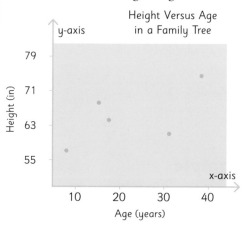

A scatter diagram comparing the height versus age in a family of five.

scientific notation

A quick and easy way of writing very big or very small numbers using powers of ten.

$$10{,}352 = 1.0352 \times 10^4$$

This tells us that the decimal point must move 4 places to the right.

$$1{,}300{,}000 = 1.3 \times 10^6$$

This tells us that the decimal point must move six places to the right.

See **power (of a number)**

score

The amount of points gained or grade made in a competition or test.

TEST			
1	6+1=7 ✔	6	5+5=10 ✔
2	3+3=6 ✔	7	3+1=5 ✘
3	5-2=3 ✔	8	3+7=10 ✔
4	10-2=7 ✘	9	1+8=9 ✔
5	10-7=3 ✔	10	4+4=8 ✔

Score = $^8/_{10}$

See **average, mean, median, mode**

second

The ordinal number (one that indicates position) that comes after first (1st).

1st   2nd

See **ordinal number**

second

See **time**

section

1. A flat surface obtained by cutting through a solid in any direction.

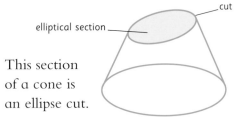

cut

elliptical section

This section of a cone is an ellipse cut.

2. When the cut is parallel to the base or side of the solid, it is called a cross-section.

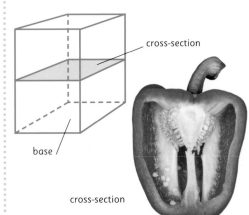

cross-section

base

cross-section

cross-section

See **cone, cross-section of a solid, ellipse, flat, segment, solid, surface**

sector

A part of a circle enclosed by two radii and an arc. The radii cut the circle into two sectors. The larger area is called the major sector; the smaller is called the minor sector.
See **arc, circle, radius**

segment

A part, a section of something.

Examples

1. A line segment.

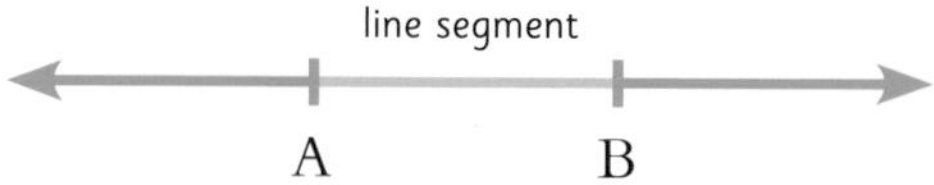

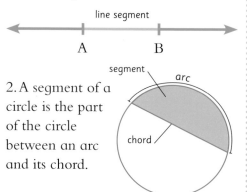

2. A segment of a circle is the part of the circle between an arc and its chord.

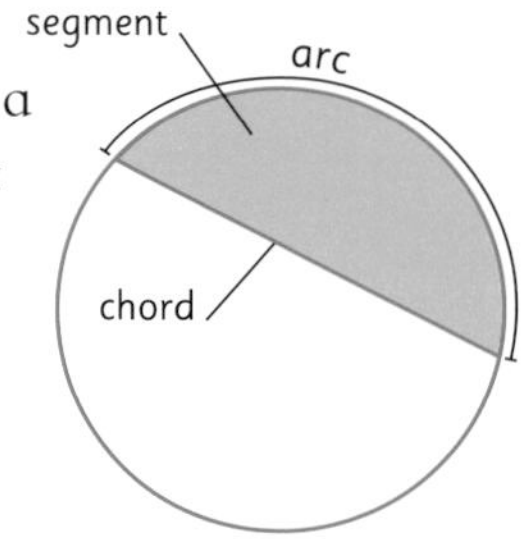

See **arc, circle**

selling price

Price at which something is sold.

Example

A car dealer sells a car for $12,000. The selling price of the car is $12,000.

See **cost price, loss, profit**

semicircle

Half a circle. When you cut a circle along its diameter, you get two semicircles.

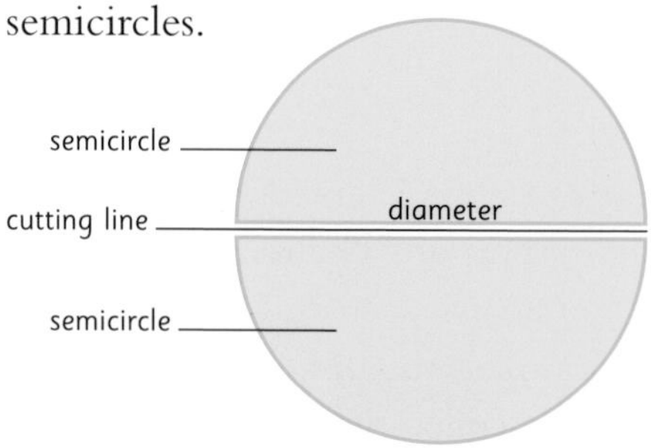

See **circle, diameter**

sentence

A statement. In mathematics a sentence may contain numerals, operators, variables, and other symbols.

Examples

$$2x + y = 6$$
$$2x > 6$$

See **false sentence, number sentence, numeral, open number sentence, pronumeral, true sentence**

sequence

A set of numbers or a pattern following an order or rule.

Examples

1, 3, 5, 7, 9, 11...

1. The rule of this sequence is "add 2."

2. In the sequence below, each shape is following a pattern of rotation counterclockwise by the same amount of turn.

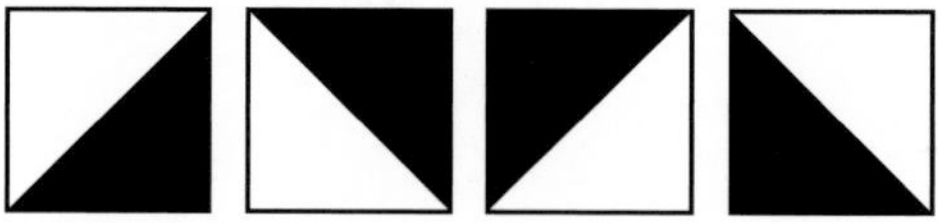

See **counterclockwise, order, pattern, progression, rotation, rule**

set

Symbol { }

A group of objects or numbers.
Each object in a set is called a
member or an element of the set.
The elements of a set are written
inside braces { }.

Example

Set of whole numbers
= {0, 1, 2, 3, 4…}

See **element of a set**

set triangle

An instrument used for geometrical
drawings.

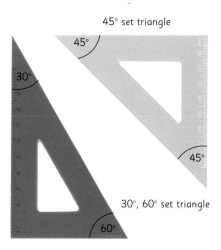

45° set triangle

45°

30°

45°

30°, 60° set triangle

60°

Set triangles are used for drawing
parallel lines and angles.

See **parallel lines, right angle**

shape

The form of an object. Two-
dimensional (2-D) shapes include
triangles, quadrilaterals, polygons.

Three-dimensional (3-D) shapes
include cubes, prisms, and pyramids.

See **cube, dimension, prism,
pyramid, quadrilateral,
three-dimensional, triangle,
two-dimensional**

sharing

See **division**

side

A line segment that is a part of
a perimeter or of a figure.

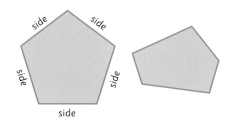

side   side

side   side

side

A pentagon has five sides.

See **line segment, pentagon,
perimeter**

side view

A diagram, as seen from the side.

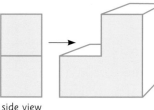
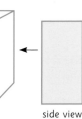

side view   side view

See **cross-section of a solid,
front view, plan**

a
b
c
d
e
f
g
h
i
j
k
l
m
n
o
p
q
r
s
t
u
v
w
x
y
z

sign

A symbol used in math instead
of words. Some of the main signs are:

✚	**Addition**
━	**Subtraction**
✖	**Multiplication**
➗	**Division**
═	**Equals**
%	**Percentage**
>	**Greater than**
<	**Less than**

See **operation**

significant figure

A digit in a number that is
considered important when rounding
numbers up or down or when
making an approximation.

3,745 rounded to two significant figures is **3,700**

0.165m rounded to one significant figure is **0.2m**

See **approximation, digit,
rounding**

similar

The same in shape but not in size.
Two shapes are similar figures if the
corresponding angles are equal and
all sides are enlarged or reduced by
the same ratio.

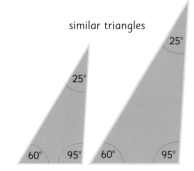

similar triangles

See **congruent, enlarge, ratio,
reduce**

simplify

To write something in the simplest,
shortest form.
Example
The fractions below have
been simplified by making the
numerator and denominator
as small as possible.

$$\frac{8}{10} + \frac{4}{20} = \frac{4}{5} + \frac{1}{5} = \frac{5}{5} = 1$$

See **canceling**

size

The amount or dimensions
of something.
The size of this
angle is 37°.

37°

skew lines

Lines that do not intersect and are not
parallel, so are not on the same plane.
See **intersect, parallel lines**

slide
Change position on the surface.
See **flip, rotation, translation, turn**

slope
The slope of a line measures the steepness, or gradient, of the line. Slope is calculated by dividing the rise by the run.

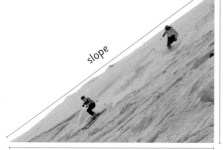

rise

run

solid
A solid is a figure with three dimensions, usually length, width, and height.

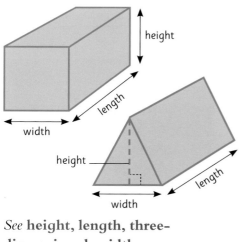

height

length

width

height

width

length

See **height, length, three-dimensional, width**

solution
The answer to a problem or question.
Example

| The equation: | $x + 4 = 9$ |
| has a solution: | $x = 5$ |

solve
Find the answer.
See **calculate, solution**

some
Not all of the whole, a part.

a whole cake

some of the cake

sorting
Putting objects that share similar features (attributes) into groups.

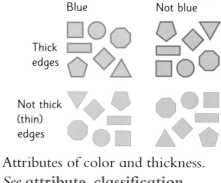

Blue   Not blue

Thick edges

Not thick (thin) edges

Attributes of color and thickness.
See **attribute, classification, diagram, group**

space

Space is any 3-D region.
spatial Things that are relating
to, or happening in, space.
Spatial figures (solids) have
three dimensions.
See **dimension, region, solid,
three-dimensional**

span

Stretch from side to side, across.
See **handspan**

speed

The rate of time at which something
travels; the distance traveled in
a unit of time.

Example
A car traveled 35 miles (60 km) in one
hour. Its speed was 35 mph (60 km/h).
See **distance, knot, unit of
measurement**

sphere

A 3-D shape like a round ball. It has
one curved surface and no corners or
edges. Every point on the sphere's
surface is the same distance from the
sphere's center.

Examples

a basketball   the Earth
See **three-dimensional**

spinner

A disk used in
chance games.
It can be spun
to produce a
random number.

spiral

A curve that goes around and around
a central point, getting farther and
farther away from it as it goes.

central point
(fixed)
See **curve**

spring balance

An instrument that
measures weight or mass.
A spring inside the
balance is stretched by
the force equal to the
mass of the object.
See **mass, weight**

square

A quadrilateral
with four equal sides
and four right angles.

See **quadrilateral, right angle**

square centimeter

Symbol cm^2
A square centimeter is a metric
unit for measuring area.

3 cm

1 cm

The area of this shape is 3 square
centimeters.

$$3 \text{ cm} \times 1 \text{ cm} = 3 \text{ cm}^2$$

See **area, unit of measurement**

square kilometer

Symbol km^2
A metric unit for measuring very
large areas, such as part of a country.

$$1 \text{ km}^2 = 1,000,000 \text{ m}^2$$

Smaller areas, such as the size of
farms, are measured in hectares.

$$1 \text{ km}^2 = 100 \text{ ha}$$

See **area, hecta, unit of
measurement**

square meter

Symbol m^2
A metric unit for measuring area.

$$1 \text{ m}^2 = 10,000 \text{ cm}^2$$

1.5 m

Example
This rug has an
area of 4.5 m^2.

3 m

See **area, square
centimeter, unit
of measurement**

square number

A number that can be represented
by dots in the shape of a square.
Examples

4   9   16

See **rectangular number, triangle
number**

square of a number

The answer you get when you
multiply a number by itself.

$$3^2 = 3 \times 3 = 9$$
$$5^2 = 5 \times 5 = 25$$

$$(0.5)^2 = 0.5 \times 0.5$$
$$= 0.25$$

See **index, square root**

square paper

Paper divided up into squares, which is used for scale drawing and drawing graphs. Square paper is also called graph paper.

Examples

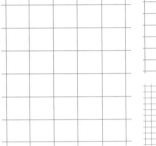

See **dot paper**

square root

A number that, when multiplied by itself, produces the given number. It is the inverse (reverse) of squaring a number.

Square root of 9 (√9) is 3
as 3 × 3 = 9

Square root of 25 (√25) is 5
as 5 × 5 = 25

See **square of a number**

standard unit of measuring

Units of measure that are internationally accepted.

See **unit of measurement**

statistics

The collection and grouping of facts in number form. The information collected is called data. Data can be shown in a table or on a graph.

Example

This table shows the favorite foods of a class of 20 children.

Meat	Vegetables	Fruit
Steve P.	Rick	Anne
John	Hirani	James
Shari	Trevor	Claire
Ramon	Sam	Ranjit
Jackie		Dean
Sarah		Steve N.
David		Belinda
Jeremy		
Darren		

From this data, we can work out percentages.

9 out of 20 children prefer meat:
$$\frac{9}{20} = 45\%$$
of the class prefers meat.

4 out of 20 children prefer vegetables:
$$\frac{4}{20} = 20\%$$
of the class prefers vegetables.

7 out of 20 children prefer fruit:
$$\frac{7}{20} = 35\%$$
of the class prefers fruit.

The percentages are statistics about the food preferences of the class.

See **data, percent**

stone

Symbol st
An Imperial unit of weight in the UK.

14 pounds (lb) = 1 stone

See **ounce, pound**

straight angle

An angle of 180°.

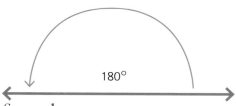

180°

See **angle**

subset

A set within a larger set.
Examples
1. If each element of set S is also an element of set T, then S is called a subset of T.
Set T = {natural numbers to 25}
Set S = {square numbers to 25}

Set T

Set S

1 11
15
20   6
14   18
19   12   4   25   10
23   5
24   3   9   16   8
21   13
2   7   22
17

2. Set A = {all children in your class}
Set B = {all girls in your class}
Set B is a subset of set A, because all the elements in set B are also in set A.
See **combination, set**

substitution

1. Something standing in place of another.
Examples

> If a = 5 and b = 2, what is the value of 2a + 2b?
> **2a + 2b = 2 × 5 + 2 × 2**
> **= 10 + 4**
> **= 14**

2. The replacement of a letter in a code message, or a place holder in a number sentence, by a number.
Example
In this secret code, numbers are substituted for letters.

A	B	C	D	E	F	G	H	...
1	2	3	4	5	6	7	8	...

2	1	4	7	5
B	A	D	G	E

See **code, number sentence, place holder**

subtraction

subtract, subtracting
Symbol −

1. Taking away (finding what is left).
Jane had 5 pencils
and gave 3 to Jon.
How many pencils
does Jane have left?

$$5 - 3 = 2$$

Jane has 2 pencils.

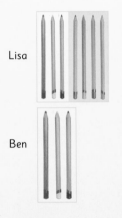

Lisa

Ben

2. Difference
(comparison).
Lisa has 7 pencils
and Ben has
3 pencils. How
many more
pencils than Ben
does Lisa have?

$$7 - 3 = 4$$

Lisa has 4 more pencils than Ben.

3. Complementary addition
(counting on to see how many
are missing).
Andy has 3 pencils,
but needs 7. How
many more must
he get?

$$3 + 4 = 7$$

Andy must get 4 more pencils.

Subtraction may
be represented on
a number line.
Example

$$5 - 3 = 2$$

Show on a number line:

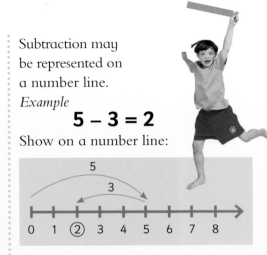

repeated subtraction Repeatedly
taking away the same number from
a given number until you reach zero.
Example
You want to give 20 books to five
friends. You give one book to each
friend, then another book to each
until there are no books left:

$$20 - 5 - 5 - 5 - 5 = 0$$

We have subtracted 5 from 20
four times:

$$20 \div 4 = 5$$

subtrahend A number that is
to be subtracted from another
number.

$$12 - 4 = 8$$

minuend ↑   ↑   ↑ difference
         subtrahend

See **difference, minuend,
number line**

sum

The answer to an addition problem. It is the total amount when you add together two or more numbers (called addends) or quantities.

Example

$$3 + 4 = 7$$

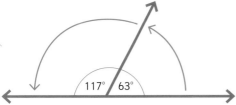

addends   sum

See **addition**

supplementary angles

Two angles that together make 180°.

117°　63°

Angles 117° and 63° are supplementary angles.
Angle 117° is called the supplement of 63°.
And angle 63° is called the supplement of 117°.
See **angle, degree**

surface

1. The outside of something.
Example
The surface of the tennis ball is furry.

2. The top level of a liquid.
Example
Plants float on the surface of a lake.

The surface of an object may be flat or curved.

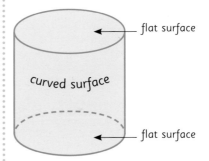

flat surface

curved surface

flat surface

A cylinder has two flat surfaces and one curved surface.

symmetry

A shape has symmetry or is symmetrical when one half of the shape can fit exactly over the other half. Shapes are called symmetrical if they have one or more lines (axes) of symmetry.
See **asymmetry, axis, line of symmetry, rotational symmetry**

Tt

table

1. An arrangement of letters or numbers in rows or columns.

×	1	2	3	4	5	6
1	1	2	3	4	5	6
2	2	4	6	8	10	12
3	3	6	9	12	15	18
4	4	8	12	16	20	24
5	5	10	15	20	25	30
6	6	12	18	24	30	36

2. When multiplication answers are arranged in order, they are called multiplication tables.

Example

The nine times table:

$1 \times 9 = 9$ $7 \times 9 = 63$

$2 \times 9 = 18$ $8 \times 9 = 72$

$3 \times 9 = 27$ $9 \times 9 = 81$

$4 \times 9 = 36$ $10 \times 9 = 90$

$5 \times 9 = 45$ $11 \times 9 = 99$

$6 \times 9 = 54$ $12 \times 9 = 108$

See **multiplication**

take away

remove, subtract

To find the difference between two numbers by removing (subtracting) one number from another. Also called subtraction.

Example

I had 15 marbles, but I lost 7 of them. How many do I have now?

$$15 - 7 = 8$$

15 take away 7 leaves eight. I have 8 marbles left.

See **subtraction**

tally

A way of counting things by making a mark for each item. The marks are usually drawn in groups of five. The fifth mark in each group crosses the other four to make them easy to count.

a tally of 13 items

tangram

A Chinese puzzle made up of a square cut into seven pieces that can be rearranged to make many different shapes.

tape measure

A strip of tape or thin metal marked with inches and centemeters.

temperature

How hot or how cold something is. Temperature is measured in degrees Fahrenheit (°F) or degrees Celsius (°C).

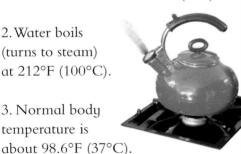

1. Water freezes (changes to ice) at 32°F (0°C).

2. Water boils (turns to steam) at 212°F (100°C).

3. Normal body temperature is about 98.6°F (37°C).

See **Celsius, Fahrenheit, thermometer**

template

A piece of cardboard or plastic for drawing shapes. It may be one of two types:

1. A solid piece of cardboard or plastic that we draw around.

using a dish as a template

2. A sheet of cardboard or firm plastic out of which shapes have been cut. This is also called a stencil.

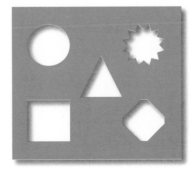

tens

A group of ten things or ten people.
ten thousand Ten lots of a thousand; 10,000.
tenth $\frac{1}{10}$
ten thousandth $\frac{1}{10,000}$

term

1. Each of the two amounts (quantities) in a ratio or a fraction.

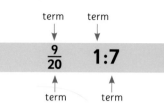

2. Each of the quantities connected by + or − in an algebraic expression or equation.

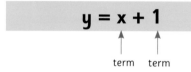

$$y = x + 1$$

term   term

See **algebra, equation**

terminate

To come to an end, finish, to go no further.

terminating decimal

A decimal fraction that is not recurring (continuing). It has an "end."
Example

$$\begin{array}{r} 0.25 \\ 4{\overline{\smash{\big)}\,1.00}} \end{array}$$

See **decimal, fraction, recurring decimal**

tessellation

tessellate

A group of identical shapes in a repeating pattern, with no overlapping or gaps between them. Regular mosaic and pavement shapes tessellate.

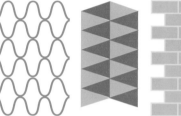

Shapes that can cover a surface completely, like squares, equilateral triangles, and hexagons, are said to tessellate.

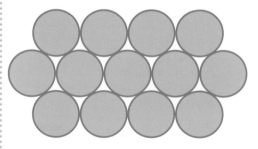

Circles do not tessellate.

See **circle, pattern, plane, square, triangle**

tetragon

A 2-D shape with four sides and four angles.
See **quadrilateral**

tetrahedron

A solid (polyhedron) with four faces. Also called a triangular pyramid. A regular tetrahedron is made of four identical (congruent) equilateral triangles.

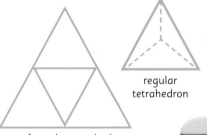

net of regular tetrahedron

regular tetrahedron

See **polyhedron**

thermometer

An instrument for measuring temperature. This thermometer shows a temperature of 71°F (22°C).
See **Celsius, temperature**

third

1. The ordinal number that comes after second and before fourth.
Example He came third in the race.

1st   2nd   3rd   4th

3rd

2. One-third means one of three equal parts. Written as $\frac{1}{3}$.

$\frac{1}{3}$	$\frac{1}{3}$	$\frac{1}{3}$

$\frac{1}{3}$ has been colored in.

See **fraction, ordinal number**

thousand

Ten hundreds, written as 1,000.
See **billion, hundred, million, whole numbers**

thousandth

One part out of a thousand.

$$\tfrac{1}{1000} = 1 \text{ divided by } 1000$$

three-dimensional

3-D

When something has length, width, and height, it is said to have three dimensions and is called three-dimensional. Solids are three-dimensional.

height

width

length

See **dimension, solid, sphere**

time

A way of measuring a particular point in the day or how long something lasts. It helps us measure the past, the present, and the future.

It is 2 o'clock.

2:00

1 hour = 60 mins

It is quarter past 2.

2:15

$\frac{1}{4}$ hour = 15 mins

It is half past 2.

2:30

$\frac{1}{2}$ hour = 30 mins

60 seconds = 1 minute
60 minutes = 1 hour
24 hours = 1 day
7 days = 1 week
52 weeks = 1 year
12 months = 1 year

12-hour time A period of one day divided into two halves of 12 hours each: a.m. is from 12 o'clock midnight to 12 o'clock noon; p.m. is from noon to midnight.

a 24-hour clock

24-hour time A period of one day divided into 24 hourly divisions, to prevent errors between a.m. and p.m. times.

a.m. A term used in 12-hour time. It stands for "ante meridiem," which means "before noon."
Example The time is five past five in the morning. It is 5:05 a.m.

p.m. A term used in 12-hour time. It stands for "post meridiem," which means "after noon."

chronological order Events arranged by the date or time when they happened.

time interval The time that passes between two events.

time line A line on which events are recorded in chronological order. *Example*

Russian dog Laika is first living being to orbit Earth	Yuri Gagarin is first human in space	Neil Armstrong is first man on the Moon	Valentina Tereshkova is first woman in space
1957	**1961**	**1969**	**1978**

times

Another word for "multiplied by."
See **multiplication**

ton

symbol t
A metric ton is a unit for measuring the amount of material that an object contains (mass). One metric ton = 1,000 kg. One Imperial ton = 2,000 lb.

The mass of this truck is 1.435 tons or 1,435 kilograms.
See **kilo, liter, mass, metric system**

torus

A round 3-D shape with a hole in the middle, like a doughnut or a tire tube.

total

1. Sum. When you add things or values together, the answer is the total.

$$10 + 20 + 25 = 55$$

2. Whole.
See **addition, sum**

transformation

transform
1. Changing the shape, position, or size of an object. This may be done by enlargement, rotation, reflection, or translation.
2. Changing a number or equation to a different form, but with the same result.

$$\frac{1}{2} = 0.5 = 50\%$$

See **enlarge, flip, one-to-one correspondence, projection, reduce, reflection, rotation, translation**

translate

translation
To move a shape without lifting it, rotating it, or reflecting it.

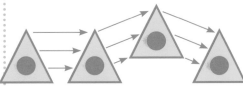

See **flip, reflection, rotation, slide, turn**

trapezium

A quadrilateral with no parallel sides.

trapezoid

A four-sided shape (quadrilateral) with one pair of sides parallel and the other pair of sides not parallel.

See **parallel lines, quadrilateral**

treble; triple

Make three times bigger or multiply by three.

See **multiplication**

tree diagram

A diagram that has a branchlike structure and shows all possible outcomes.

Example

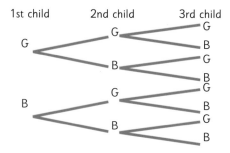

1st child   2nd child   3rd child

If a family has three children, they may have a boy, then a girl, then a boy; or a girl, then a boy, then a boy, etc. There are 8 possible outcomes.

triangle

A polygon with three sides and three angles. We can classify triangles by sides or by angles. The sum of angles inside a triangle is always 180°.

Examples

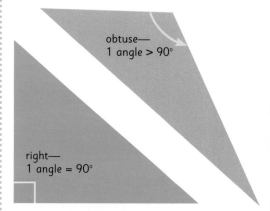

1. By sides:

equilateral— 3 sides equal

isosceles— 2 sides equal

scalene—all sides different in length

2. By angles:

obtuse— 1 angle > 90°

right— 1 angle = 90°

See **equilateral, isosceles triangle, plane, right angle, scalene triangle, sum**

triangle number

triangular number

A number that can be represented by dots in the shape of a triangle.

Examples

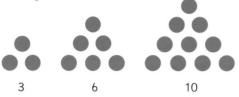

3   6   10

See **triangle**

trillion

A trillion is a million million:

1,000,000,000,000

10^{12}

In some European countries, a trillion is a million million million.

true sentence

A sentence about numbers that is true or correct.

Examples

$3 \times 2 = 2 \times 3$ is a true sentence.

$6 \neq 5$ is a true sentence.

The open number sentence

$2 + x = 9$

becomes true if x is replaced by 7.

If x is replaced by any other number, then it will become a false sentence.

See **false sentence, number sentence, open number sentence**

turn

To move or change position by rotating.

See **rotation**

twice

Two times, or double.

Example

Twelve is worth twice as much as six.

two-dimensional

2-D

When something has length and width, then it has two dimensions and is two-dimensional. Plane shapes and surfaces have two dimensions.

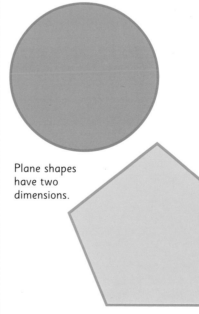

Plane shapes have two dimensions.

See **dimension, length, plane, region, surface, width**

a b c d e f g h i j k l m n o p q r s **t** u v w x y z

unequal

Symbol ≠
Not equal.

$$3 \neq 4$$

This equation says:
"Three is not equal to four."
See **inequality**

union

A combination of two or
more things.

vegetables

red objects

In this Venn diagram, pepper is
the union of the sets of vegetables
and red objects.
See **set, Venn diagram**

unit fraction

A fraction with a numerator and
denominator that are whole numbers.
Also called a simple or common fraction.

numerator → $\dfrac{3}{4}$ ← denominator

See **fraction**

unit price

The price at which something
is produced or bought.
Example
A car dealer buys a car for $10,000.
The unit price, or cost price, of the
car is $10,000.

unit of measurement

Units we use when measuring things
Standard units are
the same sizes
across the world.

A **minute** is a
unit of time.

The minute hand
is pointing to 12.

A **kilometer** is a metric unit
that measures distance.

The Golden Gate
Bridge in California
is 1 kilometer long.

unit square

A square with each side equal to one unit of length or distance.

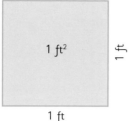

1 ft²

1 ft

1 ft

A square with sides one foot long has an area of one square foot (1 ft²).

See **area, distance, length, unit of measurement**

A **gram** is a unit of mass.

500 grams of flour

Other units include liter (to measure volume) and Celsius (temperature).
See **metric system, standard unit of measuring**

unknown value

An amount that is not known. In mathematical sentences, unknown values are represented by symbols or letters called pronumerals or variables.

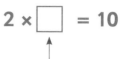

$$2 \times \square = 10$$

unknown value

$$3a - 2b = 12$$

unknown value

See **pronumeral, variable**

unlike terms

Terms that are not like. Unlike terms cannot be combined or simplified by adding or subtracting.

2 pineapples + 2 bananas

These fruits are unlike terms, so they cannot be combined to find an answer.

$$2a + 3b \qquad 2a + a$$

unlike terms   like terms

See **like terms**

a b c d e f g h i j k l m n o p q r s t **u** v w x y z

value

The value of something is what it is worth.

1. The value of $3 + 5 = 8$.
2. The vase costs $80.
Its value is $80.
3. Things of equal value are worth the same. $1 has the same value as 100 cents.

See **evaluate**

vanishing point

The point or points in perspective drawings where all parallel lines appear to meet.

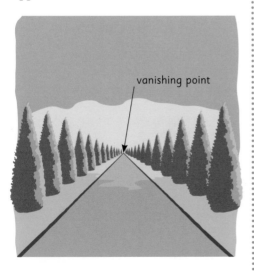

vanishing point

See **perspective**

variable

A symbol or letter that represents an unknown member of a set. Sometimes it is called an unknown or a pronumeral.

$$x + 2 = 5$$

x is the variable

See **constant, number sentence, open number sentence, place holder, pronumeral**

Venn diagram

A Venn diagram is used to sort things into groups or sets. It shows how the sets are related. It is named after Englishman John Venn, who invented it.

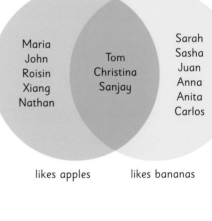

Maria
John
Roisin
Xiang
Nathan

Tom
Christina
Sanjay

Sarah
Sasha
Juan
Anna
Anita
Carlos

likes apples   likes bananas

This Venn diagram shows that Tom, Christina, and Sanjay like both apples and bananas.

See **diagram, set**

vertex

Plural vertices

1. The top; the highest part or point. The vertex is the point opposite the base.
2. A point where two or more adjacent lines meet to form a corner or angle.

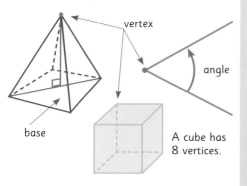

vertex

angle

base

A cube has 8 vertices.

See **adjacent, apex**

vertical

A vertical line is at a right angle (perpendicular) to the horizon.

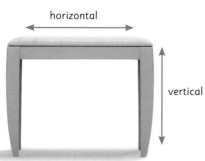

horizontal

vertical

The top of a table is horizontal. The legs of a table are vertical.
See **horizontal line, perpendicular, right angle**

vertically opposite angles

When two lines cross, they make four angles at the point where they meet. The angles opposite from each other are equal in size and are called vertically opposite angles.

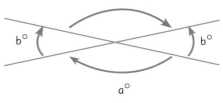

a°

b°   b°

a°

See **angles, parallel lines, vertex**

volume

The amount of space inside a container, or the actual amount of material in the container.

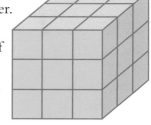

The volume of this object is 27 cubic units.

Some units of volume are:
For solids: cubic centimeter (cm³), cubic meter (m³), cubic inch (in³)
For liquids: liter (l), pint (p), gallon (g)
See **capacity, cubic unit**

a
b
c
d
e
f
g
h
i
j
k
l
m
n
o
p
q
r
s
t
u
v
w
x
y
z

Ww

week

A period of 7 days.

weight

How heavy something is. Weight is the pull of gravity (a force of attraction) on an object. The weight of an object changes if gravitational pull changes, but its mass (the amount of matter it is made of) always remains the same.

Astronauts become weightless in space but the mass of their bodies does not change.

Astronaut
on Earth:
His mass = 75 kg
His weight ≈ 75 kg

Astronaut in space:
His mass is still 75 kg
but he is weightless.
People often speak incorrectly of weight when they really mean mass.
See **mass**

whole numbers

Zero together with all counting numbers, but no fractions or decimals.

See **counting, zero**

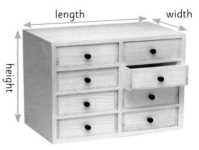

width

The measurement of something from side to side. It is also called breadth.

length · width · height

The width of this chest of drawers is 28 in (70 cm).

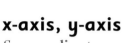

a b c d e f g h i j k l m n o p q r s t u v w x y z

x-axis, y-axis
See **coordinates**

yard
An Imperial measure of length.
1 yard = 36 inches ≈ 91 cm

year
The period of time it takes the Earth to make one complete revolution around the Sun: 365 days, 5 hours, and $48\frac{3}{4}$ minutes.
See **time, revolution**

zero
Symbols 0, Ø
The numeral 0; nothing.

Rules for working with zero:

1. A number + 0 = same number

$$5 + 0 = 5$$

2. A number − 0 = same number

$$7 - 0 = 7$$

3. A number × 0 = 0

$$6 × 0 = 0$$

4. 0 ÷ any number = 0

$$0 ÷ 10 = 0$$

5. A number ÷ 0 has no answer

$$3 ÷ 0 = \text{can't do}$$

The digit zero is used as a place holder in numerals.

In the number sixty, 0 is a place holder for units. It shows that the 6 means six tens and there are no single units.

These words all mean zero: naught, nil, none, nix, null, void, empty set, zilch, love (in tennis).

See **digit, place holder**

Quick reference

SYMBOLS

symbols	meaning	example
+	add, plus	2 + 1 = 3
-	subtract, take away, minus	7 − 6 = 1
×	multiply by, times	3 × 3 = 9
÷ ⟋	divide by	9 ÷ 2 = 4.5
=	is equals to, equals	2 + 2 = 1 + 3
≠	is not equal to	2 ≠ 5
≈ ≐ ≏	is approximately equal to	302 ≈ 300
≤	is less than or equal to	x ≤ 12
≥	is greater than or equal to	y ≥ 6
>	is greater than	7 > 6
<	is less than	2 < 4
≮	is not less than	6 ≮ 5
≯	is not greater than	3.3 ≯ 3.4
$	dollar(s)	$4.50
¢	cent(s)	50¢
£	pound(s)	£1.20
p	pence	50p
€	Euro	€5
.	decimal point (on the line)	5.24
%	percent, out of 100	50%
°	degree (temperature, angle measure)	45°F, 10°C, 90°
'	foot/feet (Imperial system)	1' = 12" (30 cm)
"	inch/inches (Imperial system)	12" = 1'
( ), { }, [ ]	parentheses, brackets	6 + (5 x 2) = 16

^{2}	squared	$3^2 = 9$
^{3}	cubed	$3^3 = 27$
$\sqrt{}$	square root	$\sqrt{9} = 3$
π	pi	π is approximately 3.14
∟	right angle, 90°	
⊥	is perpendicular to, at 90°	
⤢ ⤢	parallel lines	
\ \\	line segments of the same length	

USEFUL NUMBER WORDS

number	plural	ordinal number
1	ones	first
2	twos	second
3	threes	third
4	fours	fourth
5	fives	fifth
6	sixes	sixth
7	sevens	seventh
8	eights	eighth
9	nines	ninth
10	tens	tenth
100	hundreds	hundredth
1,000	thousands	thousandth
10,000	ten thousands	10^4
100,000	hundred thousands	10^5
1,000,000	millions	10^6
1,000,000,000	billions	10^9
1,000,000,000,000	trillions	10^{12}
1,000,000,000,000,000	quadrillion (million billions)	10^{15}

Quick reference

NUMERICAL PREFIXES

prefix	meaning	example
mono	1	monorail
bi	2	bicycle, binary
tri	3	tricycle, triangle
tetra, quad	4	tetrahedron, quadrilateral
penta, quin	5	pentagon
hexa	6	hexagon
hepta, septi	7	heptagon
octa	8	octagon
nona, non	9	nonagon
deca	10	decagon, decahedron
dodeca	12	dodecagon, dodecahedron
hect	100	hectare
kilo	1,000	kilometer, kilogram
mega	1,000,000	megaliter, megawatt
milli	$\frac{1}{1,000}$ (one thousandth)	milligram
centi	$\frac{1}{100}$ (one hundredth)	centimeter

OTHER PREFIXES

prefix	meaning	example
anti	opposite, against	counterclockwise
circum	around	circumference
co	together	cointerior, coordinate
geo	earth	geometry
hemi	half	hemisphere
macro	very big	macrocosmos
micro	very small	microbe
multi	many, much	multibase blocks
poly	many	polygon
semi	half	semicircle
sub	below, under	subset
trans	across, beyond, over	transverse
uni	one, having one	unit

LENGTH

metric

10 millimeters (mm)	= 1 centimeter (cm)
100 centimeters (cm)	= 1 meter (m)
1,000 millimeters (mm)	= 1 meter (m)
1,000 meters (m)	= 1 kilometer (km)

Imperial

12 inches (in)	= 1 foot (ft)
3 feet (ft)	= 1 yard (yd)
1,760 yards (yd)	= 1 mile
5,280 feet (ft)	= 1 mile
8 furlongs	= 1 mile

AREA

metric

100 square millimeters (mm^2)	=	1 square centimeter (cm^2)
10,000 square centimeters (cm^2)	=	1 square meter (m^2)
10,000 square meters (m^2)	=	1 hectare (ha)
100 hectares (ha)	=	1 square kilometer (km^2)
1 square kilometer (km^2)	=	1,000,000 square meters (m^2)

Imperial

144 square inches (sq in)	=	1 square foot (sq ft)
9 square feet (sq ft)	=	1 square yard (sq yd)
1,296 square inches (sq in)	=	1 square yard (sq yd)
43,560 square feet (sq ft)	=	1 acre
640 acres	=	1 square mile (sq mile)

MASS

metric

1,000 milligrams (mg)	= 1 gram (g)
1,000 grams (g)	= 1 kilogram (kg)
1,000 kilograms (kg)	= 1 tonne (t)

Imperial

16 ounces (oz)	= 1 pound (lb)
100 pounds (lb)	= 1 hundredweight
2,000 pounds (lb)	= 1 ton
20 hundredweight	= 1 ton

LIQUID VOLUME

metric

1,000 milliliters (ml) = 1 liter (l)
1 ml (for liquids) = 1 cm³ (for solids)
1,000 liters (l) = 1 kiloliter (kl)
1 kl (for liquids) = 1 m³ (for solids)

Imperial

8 fluid ounces (fl oz) = 1 cup
16 fluid ounces (fl oz) = 1 pint (pt)
2 cups (c) = 1 pint (pt)
2 pints (pt) = 1 quart (qt)
4 quarts (qt) = 1 gallon (gal)
8 pints (pt) = 1 gallon (gal)

ANGLES

1 right angle	=	90 degrees (90°)
1 straight angle	=	180 degrees (180°)
1 revolution	=	360 degrees (360°)

Conversion tables

LENGTH

metric		Imperial
1 millimeter (mm)	=	0.03937 inches (in)
1 centimeter (cm)	=	0.3937 inches (in)
1 meter (m)	=	1.0936 yards (yd)
1 kilometer (km)	=	0.6214 miles

Imperial		metric
1 inch (in)	=	2.54 centimeters (cm)
1 foot (ft)	=	0.3048 meters (m)
1 yard (yd)	=	0.9144 meters (m)
1 mile	=	1.6093 kilometers (km)
1 nautical mile	=	1.853 kilometers (km)

AREA

metric		Imperial
1 square centimeter (cm^2)	=	0.155 square inches (sq in)
1 square meter (m^2)	=	1.1960 square yards (sq yd)
1 hectare (ha)	=	2.4711 acres
1 square kilometer (km^2)	=	0.3861 square yards (sq yd)

Imperial		metric
1 square inch (sq in)	=	6.4516 square centimeters (cm^2)
1 square foot (sq ft)	=	0.0929 square meters (m^2)
1 square yard (sq yd)	=	0.8361 square meters (m^2)
1 acre	=	0.4 hectares (ha)
1 square mile (sq mile)	=	2.59 square kilometers (km^2)

MASS

metric		Imperial
1 milligram (mg)	=	0.0154 grains
1 gram (g)	=	0.0353 ounces (oz)
1 kilogram (kg)	=	2.2046 pounds (lb)
1 metric ton	=	1.102 short tons

Imperial		metric
1 ounce (oz)	=	28.35 grams (g)
1 pound (lb)	=	0.4536 kilogram (kg)
1 hundredweight	=	43.359 kilogram (kg)
1 short ton	=	0.907 metric tons

VOLUME

metric	Imperial
1 cubic centimeter (cm³)	= 0.0610 in³
1 dm³ (decimeter)/1,000 cm³	= 0.0353 ft³
1 cubic meter (m³)	= 1.3080 yd³
1 liter (l)/1 dm³	= 2.11 pint (pt)
1 hectoliter (hl)/100 l	= 26.42 gallons

Imperial	metric
1 cubic inch (in³)	= 16.387 cm³
1 ft³/1,728 in³	= 0.0283 m³
1 fluid ounce (fl oz)	= 29.574 ml
1 pint (pt)/16 fl oz	= 0.4731 l
1 gallon/8 pt	= 3.7854 l

TEMPERATURE

To convert from Celsius to Fahrenheit
Times by 9, divide by 5, and add 32 $(C \times 9) \div 5 + 32 = F$

To convert from Fahrenheit to Celsius
Minus 32, times by 5, and divide by 9 $5 \times (Fahrenheit - 32) \div 9 = C$

HOW TO CONVERT METRIC and IMPERIAL MEASURES

to change	to	multiply by
acres	hectares	0.40
centimeters	feet	0.03
centimeters	inches	0.39
feet	centimeters	30.48
feet	meters	0.30
gallons	liters	3.79
grams	ounces	0.04
hectares	acres	2.47
inches	centimeters	2.54
kilograms	pounds	2.20
kilometers	miles	0.62

to change	to	multiply by
kilometers per hour	miles per hour	0.62
liters	gallons	0.26
liters	pints	2.11
liters	quarts	1.06
meters	feet	3.28
meters	yards	1 .09
meters per minute	centimeters per second	1.66
meters per minute	feet per second	0.05
miles	kilometers	1.61
miles per hour	kilometers per hour	1.60
miles per hour	meters per second	0.45
millimeters	inches	0.04
ounces	grams	28.35
pints	liters	0.47
pounds	kilograms	0.45
quarts	liters	0.95
quarts (dry)	cubic inches	67.2
quarts (liquid)	cubic inches	57.75
square centimeters	square inches	0.16
square feet	square meters	0.09
square inches	square centimeters	6.45
square kilometers	square miles	0.38
square meters	square feet	10.76
square meters	square yards	1.19
square miles	square kilometers	2.59
square yards	square meters	0.83
tons (metric)	tons (Imperial)	1.10
tons (Imperial)	tons (metric)	0.91
yards	meters	0.91

THE MULTIPLICATION TABLE (1–12)

×	1	2	3	4	5	6	7	8	9	10	11	12
1	1	2	3	4	5	6	7	8	9	10	11	12
2	2	4	6	8	10	12	14	16	18	20	22	24
3	3	6	9	12	15	18	21	24	27	30	33	36
4	4	8	12	16	20	24	28	32	36	40	44	48
5	5	10	15	20	25	30	35	40	45	50	55	60
6	6	12	18	24	30	36	42	48	54	60	66	72
7	7	14	21	28	35	42	49	56	63	70	77	84
8	8	16	24	32	40	48	56	64	72	80	88	96
9	9	18	27	36	45	54	63	72	81	90	99	108
10	10	20	30	40	50	60	70	80	90	100	110	120
11	11	22	33	44	55	66	77	88	99	110	121	132
12	12	24	36	48	60	72	84	96	108	120	132	144

Acknowledgments

The publisher would like to thank the following for their kind permission to reproduce their photographs:

(Key: a-above; b-below/bottom; c-center; f-far; l-left; r-right; t-top)

Corbis: John Block / Brand X 55c; Burke / Triolo Productions / Brand X 66tl; Randy Faris 73cl; Joson / Zefa 8cr; Matthias Kulka / Zefa 114-115; MedioImages 36br; Steven Mark Needham / Envision 99fcr; Kelly Redinger / Design Pics 14crb; Thinkstock 47cr; Josh Westrich / Zefa 95crb. **DK Images**: Sarah Ashun 93fcra; Rick and Rachel Bufton 100cl; Jane Bull 1clb, 1crb, 1fbl, 1fbr, 6bc, 34fcl, 38cra, 62crb, 64ca, 104ftr; NASA 118c; Ray Smith 104bl, 104cl, 104cla, 104fcl; South of England Rare Breeds Centre, Ashford, Kent 72cr; Stephen Oliver 2tr, 20bl (cars), 21tr, 43tl, 55cr, 56tl. **Dreamstime.com**: 16tr, 46br (apples); 46br (bananas), 46br (cherries), 46br (oranges), 46br (pears), 91bc, 93fbl, 117bl. **Getty Images**: Allsport Concepts / Nathan Bilow 99cla; De Agostini Picture Library / DEA / C. Dani 101fcra; Image Source 19br, 72bl; Imagenavi / Sozaijiten / Datacraft 80tr; PhotoAlto Agency RF Collections / ZenShui / Laurence Mouton 71ftl, 71tc, 71tl; Photodisc 11bl; Photodisc / Amos Morgan 71br; Photodisc / C Squared Studios 26br, 26crb, 26fbr, 26fcrb; Photodisc / Don Farrall 62cl; Photodisc / Plush Studios 21br; Photodisc / Russell Illig 111bl; Photodisc / SW Productions 107bc; Photographer's Choice / Burazin 61bl; Photographer's Choice / Jose Luis Pelaez Inc 70bl; Photographer's Choice / Kevin Summers Photography 34bl (apples), 34cl (apples); Photographer's Choice / Lew Robertson 26cr, 26cra; PhotosIndia.com 63tl; Riser / David Roth 61fbl; Stockbyte 84tr; StockFood Creative / Gustavo Andrade 66ftl; StockFood Creative / Karl Newedel 86cb; Stone / Gabrielle Revere 59br; Stone / Stuart McClymont 82bl; Stone+ / Diego Uchitel 50cla; Taxi / Space Frontiers / Dera 100ftr; Westend61 / Creativ Studio Heinemann 45cr. **iStockphoto.com**: 45RPM 76br; bbszabi 49clb; Graham Klotz 61cr.

All other images © **Dorling Kindersley**
For further information see: **www.dkimages.com**